COMING HOME
Stories of Anabaptists
in
Britain and Ireland

COMING HOME
Stories of Anabaptists
in Britain and Ireland

Edited by
Alan Kreider
and
Stuart Murray

PUBLISHED BY PANDORA PRESS
KITCHENER, ONTARIO
CO-PUBLISHED WITH HERALD PRESS
SCOTTDALE, PENNSYLVANIA

Canadian Cataloguing in Publication Data

Coming home : stories of Anabaptists in Britain and Ireland

Includes bibliographical references.
ISBN 0-9685543-6-9

1. Anabaptists – England. 2. Anabaptists – Ireland. 3. Anabaptists –
England – History. I. Kreider, Alan, 1941- II. Murray, Stuart, 1956-

BX 4933.E5C66 2000   284'.3   C00-931255-2

COMING HOME: STORIES OF ANABAPTISTS IN BRITAIN AND IRELAND
Copyright © 2000 by Pandora Press
51 Pandora Avenue North
Kitchener, Ontario, N2H 3C1
All rights reserved.

Copublished with Herald Press,
Scottdale, Pennsylvania/Waterloo, Ontario

International Standard Book Number: 0-9685543-6-9
Printed in Canada on acid-free paper.

Design by Nathan Stark
Cover illustration from a painting by Bill Downey, commissioned by the city
of Kitchener, Ontario. It is used here with permission.
The engraving by Jan Luyken on page 8 used with permission of Conrad
Grebel College archives.

10 09 08 07 06 05 04 03 02 01 00 12 11 10 9 8 7 6 5 4 3 2 1

TABLE OF CONTENTS

PART II ESSAYS AND REFLECTIONS

Dirk Willems turns to rescue his captor.
An engraving by Jan Luyken,
from the *Martyrs Mirror.*

Dirk Willems:
An Example to Others

Alan Kreider

In 1569 - four hundred and thirty years ago – Dirk Willems turned back. Within a couple of months of his dramatic action he was burned at the stake for heresy. And ever since, his life and death – made visual in Jan Luyken's engraving which freezes the moment of his turning – have had an astonishing impact.

Dirk was a young man from the town of Asperen in the Netherlands.[1] As a teenager he met some Anabaptists. Their vision of Christian discipleship gripped his imagination, and he was (re)baptised in the neighbouring city of Rotterdam. Returning to Asperen, he – according to the legal document which sentenced him to death – in his house "harbored and admitted secret conventicles and prohibited doctrines." That is, Dirk took part in a church that met illicitly in his home where he and others taught a way of being Christian that was unacceptable to the Roman Catholic church which, backed up by Spanish military might, was trying to hold on to power. Dirk was arrested and imprisoned. But he managed to escape from the prison – he climbed out a window and clambered down a rope made of knotted cloths – and he ran for safety. It was early spring; as he approached a still-frozen pond a guard was chasing him. Dirk, who had been eating prison food, made it across the cracking ice. The guard had been eating rather better and broke through the ice.

In terror he cried out for help.

Dirk turned back reflexively. At great risk, he reached across the ice to rescue his pursuer, who promptly rearrested Dirk. Why did the guard do that? Was the local burgomaster watching, as one account indicates, shouting out that the guard must "consider his oath?" For whatever reason, the guard re-imprisoned Dirk in a more secure prison in the tower of the Asperen parish church. This time there was to be no escape. Dirk was tried for heresy and, according to the official death sentence, was condemned to be burned to death "for an example to others." For good measure, his property was to be confiscated "for the benefit of his royal majesty." The execution was exceptionally painful. The fire, blown by the wind away from his upper body, did its work slowly. People in the neighbouring town of Leerdam are recorded to have heard Dirk cry out over seventy times, "O, my Lord, my God."

In Asperen today there is a Dirk Willemsz Straat, along which people can walk in his memory. James C. Juhnke has written a play – *Dirk's Exodus* – making his experience come alive both for readers and in the theatre. The Luyken engraving of his turning has appeared in over 130 publications. But the true effect of Dirk's short life is on the lives of countless Christians, including many of the people who tell their stories in this book. Dirk's life has been, in the words of the people who sentenced him to death, "an example to others." And over it all linger the questions – Why did Dirk turn back? Was it right for him to turn back? Would I have turned back?

Notes

[1] The sources for this account are: Thieleman J. Van Braght, *The Bloody Theater or Martyrs Mirror of the Defenseless Christians* (Scottdale, PA: Herald Press, 1950), 741-2; John S. Oyer and Robert S. Kreider, *Mirror of the Martyrs* (Intercourse, PA: Good Books, 1990), 36-37; David Luthy, "Dirk Willems: His Noble Deed Lives On," *Family Life* (February 1995), 19-22; James C. Juhnke, *Dirk's Exodus: A Historical Drama*, in R.J. Buckman and R.N. Lawson, eds., *Four Class Acts*: Kansas Theatre (Topeka, KS: Woodley Memorial Press, Washburn University, 1992), 85-183.

Introduction

Alan Kreider and Stuart Murray

Anabaptism and the British Isles today – for most people these simply do not go together. The historically conscious may think of Anabaptism as a radical part of the European Reformation; but that was four hundred and fifty years ago, on the continent. Others who are visually aware, or who have been tourists, may think of Anabaptism as alive in the late twentieth century, but in North America where communities of photogenic Amish, Mennonites and Hutterians live. But Anabaptism in Britain and Ireland today? That seems difficult to imagine.

It's not hard to explain this silence. From the 1530s onwards in England, Anabaptism was a word of shame and abuse. It became the great pejorative, the A-word of the sixteenth and seventeenth centuries, which could categorise and discredit anyone who was more radical religiously than oneself. Anabaptists who strayed onto British soil were persecuted repeatedly. Even the Baptists, the tradition which has been most closely associated with Anabaptism, have been of two minds about the association. As Baptist theologian Nigel Wright has put it, "When Baptists want to appear respectable they talk about their Puritan roots; when they want to appear radical they talk about their Anabaptist heritage." And most of the time most Baptists have wanted to appear respectable! As a result, since the sixteenth century, Anabaptism has largely been absent from the British Isles, and its ideas, to which some radicals have now and then paid homage, have lacked embodiment in individuals and communities.

But things are changing. In the past two decades individual Christians – and even a few communities – throughout the British Isles have been discovering Anabaptism as a source of ideas, identity and a living heritage. This book is a product of that change. It grew out of something that would have been unthinkable until recently – an Anabaptist Theological Circle. This group twice a year brings together a dozen Baptist, Anglican, New Church and Mennonite theologians. To its October 1997 meeting came a request from church leaders, especially Baptists in England, for guidelines to present to congregations who are exploring Anabaptist-flavoured church renewal. What does Anabaptism have to contribute to the future of the church in England, and specifically to congregations involved in mission?

The Theological Circle was grinding away, trying to distil Anabaptist insights into a few pithy statements. Suddenly someone said, "I don't think we're doing this in a very helpful way. It doesn't feel very Anabaptist to me; it feels more like the mainstream Reformers. How about if, instead of stating normative characteristics, we decided to collect our stories? If we did, the picture of Anabaptism in the British Isles that would emerge might be less coherent; but it would be a lot more concrete – and certainly more interesting." This led to some uncomfortable hours. It seemed to divert us from the request that responsible people who care about the future of the church had made to the group. Could we instead try something very different, which might result in something unpredictably creative?

The group decided to go for the stories. An invitation to write "Anabaptist stories" was inserted in the Anabaptist Network journal, *Anabaptism Today*. The brief was simple: to tell in story form how they discovered Anabaptist thinking and how it shaped their lives and thinking. What ideas, what books, what communities were important to them in their discovery of Anabaptism? Over twenty stories arrived, some of which were from people whom we editors had not met before but who obviously are deeply affected by Anabaptism. Alan and Eleanor Kreider then wrote to other people whom they knew had been involved in the Anabaptist Network, and the collection of stories more than doubled in size.

It quickly emerged that many of the stories had a common theme – *coming home* – a phrase that cropped up so frequently in conversations that we have chosen it as the title for this book. People from an astonishing range of denominational and theological backgrounds felt that in discovering Anabaptism they were finding their home. Something clicked, something made sense, "the penny dropped," to enable people in the fluid cultural and religious situations of the late 1990s to sense that here, in Anabaptism, they belong.

Many things have no doubt led to this, but one stands out – the collapse of Christendom. For fifteen hundred years after the conversion of the Roman Emperor Constantine I in the early fourth century, Christians in the West sensed that they were a part of an all-embracing

Christian civilisation. In theory, and to a considerable extent in practice, everyone belonged to this – they were baptised into the established churches as infants, everyone believed the doctrine that orthodox Christianity prescribed, and everyone knew how Christians were supposed to behave. Of course, things were never as neat as this; the court records of Christian Europe are full of all manner of deviance. But the point is that it is the court records that inform us of this. People who dissented from the patterns of belonging, belief and behaviour of Christendom got in trouble. Christendom was powerful, but it was always questionable whether its power was rooted as much in the freely-given consent of the people as it was in inducement and compulsion.

By the post-World War II period it was clear that, in many European countries, Christendom was in crisis. Social and legal sanctions were disappearing, and people were behaving in ways that were unacceptable by the standards of Christendom. Parents were not having their babies christened; teenagers were not being confirmed; on television people began to use bad language and to despise religion. The sense of religious "at-homeness" that Christendom had provided for many people for over a millennium was now disappearing.

Christian people have responded to this in many ways. Some have sought to fight the changes in the courts, invoking "blasphemy" laws. Others have sought comfort in the spirit of the Christendom heritage – it is impressive that repeatedly in recent years records of Gregorian chant have topped the charts. Still others have prayed for "revival" or "renewal" – words which indicate a restoration of the Christendom era in which Christians could set the moral tone for the nation. Many Christians have with great energy founded new churches, experimented with new forms of worship and organised new initiatives for evangelism. As a new millennium begins, there are many who are perplexed, and who wonder about the way forward.

It is in this post-Christendom world that people have begun to "come home." They have begun to discover Anabaptism as a means of charting a distinctive way of being Christian in the British Isles. The stories of what drew some of these people to Anabaptism are the heart of this book. But central to them all is the sense that there can be a radicalism in the present through a rediscovery of a living past. Roots, actually as well as etymologically, can be radical! In many and various ways, for these people Anabaptist ideas have come as a relief, a tonic, a new way of thinking about and living the Christian mission which has special relevance for a post-Christendom world. As the stories will indicate, the result can be one of relief and gratitude. "Once no people, now God's people." This old biblical theme resounds through these stories. People who have been rootless have found roots; people who have been homeless have found a home.

For most of these people "home" is not a new denomination. There are two explicitly Anabaptist traditions represented in the UK. The Bruderhof, who have two flourishing communities in the southeast of England, have influenced many through their hospitality, the solid wooden toys which they manufacture, and their journal, *The Plough*. There are also the Mennonites, whose Wood Green Mennonite Church and London Mennonite Centre, both in North London, have provided teaching and resources. These have influenced many, and some British people have joined the Bruderhof or the Mennonites.

But many people who are drawn to Anabaptism do not want to join a new community or denomination; instead they want to graft Anabaptist understandings on to their existing church commitments. These people may well be participants in the Anabaptist Network, readers of *Anabaptism Today* or members of one of the several Anabaptist Network Study Groups meeting in different parts of the country. Most will seek to incorporate Anabaptist concerns into the lives of their Anglican parishes or New Church congregations. A few will be in a position to go further. They may be in churches which are interested in espousing Anabaptism explicitly, becoming "hyphenated-Anabaptist" congregations. Newly-planted churches may also espouse an Anabaptist identity. In the years to come, congregations that call themselves "Anabaptist-Baptist" or "Anabaptist-Wesleyan" may not seem a total oddity. But for all of these people, there is a deep expectation that the church that will survive in the post-Christendom British Isles will be a church that embodies many Anabaptist themes.

We co-editors find this fascinating. For some years we have been involved in these developments, and they intrigue us and give us hope. Our desire is that the stories which this volume contains will provoke thought and possibly even energise new initiatives – on both sides of the Atlantic and further afield. There must be many messages which the renascent Anabaptism of the British Isles will communicate to Christians in the Old and New Worlds. We will mention only a few of them.

To Christians in North America

• *"New Anabaptists" and the Holy Spirit.* In the British Isles there are Christians, neither Mennonite nor Hutterite, who have espoused Anabaptism and made it their own. They have also said, not least through the title of their journal *Anabaptism Today*, that Anabaptism has relevance in the life of contemporary Christians. What is it that draws them to Anabaptism? What insights, given their very different backgrounds, do they bring to an understanding of the sixteenth-century Anabaptists? Or to the mission of the church today? The stories make clear that a wide variety of people have discovered a great diversity of points of relevance in Anabaptism. But one thing stands out in the stories: a significant proportion of the neo-Anabaptists of Britain are charismatic Christians. Does this explain the fact that a number of them, in studying the Anabaptists of the Reformation period, are able to find dimensions of Spirit-inspired life that we conventionally call "charismatic"? What difference, North American Anabaptists might ask themselves, does the Holy Spirit make to our following of Jesus, or to our interpretation of the Bible?

• *The centrality of worship and prayer.* The Anabaptist Network in Britain has not seen itself as an academic enterprise. The Network has its quota of PhDs alongside other Christians who have no academic qualifications; but its meetings have always been concerned with practice, and they have been characterised by worship and prayer. Does this reflect the background of the British Isles Anabaptists, many of whom have been some sort of Evangelical? Or does it indicate that they are aware that they cannot follow Jesus radically and faithfully in making peace, justice and community unless God is real and they are walking in personal fellowship with Jesus in the Spirit? There seems to be a "gracefulness" among British Anabaptists which we believe is a gift of God. For North American Mennonites, whose piety has at times been severe and legalistic, there may be something to ponder here.

• *New ways of being Anabaptist.* To Christians in the British Isles Anabaptism is not old hat. It can, to be sure, be domesticated, turned into a way of talking when one wants to feel radical. But, at its best, it keeps challenging British Christians to experiment with new ways of being Christian. Anabaptism keeps raising issues about life, power and community, and these issues will not go away; and it keeps pointing to Jesus, whose words and wounds and way keep calling to adventure and risk, and keep suggesting new ways of dealing with intractable human problems. Anabaptists in the British Isles tend to be exceptionally Jesus-focussed. Is this perhaps why they are often restlessly and sacrificially committed to finding unconventional solutions to age-old problems?

• *Gratitude.* Repeatedly, the "new Anabaptists" in the British Isles express their gratitude to the old Anabaptist traditions. They are grateful to the Bruderhof for their courage and their faithfulness in incarnating a communitarian Anabaptist vision. They are grateful to North American Mennonites for the work of scholars such as John Howard Yoder, and for sending a succession of gifted staff members to the London Mennonite Centre. They would wish, we are sure, for us to use this introduction to say "Thank you!"

To Christians in the British Isles

• *The search for roots.* British Christians have for some time sensed that they can gain new insight from the groups that their predecessors persecuted and swept to the fringes. Chief among these are the Celtic Christians, about whose prayers and style of church life and mission there are many books. It is fascinating to see how descendants of the persecutors find life-giving insights in the writings of the persecuted. The parallels between the Anabaptists and the Celtic traditions are worth exploring. Both groups were marginalised by powerful religious bodies, but both are now emerging to demonstrate, to the post-Christendom world, that there is life in the roots! In contrast to the Celts, there have been few British books about the Anabaptists. The current book indicates that this neglect is now ending. Might a similar rediscovery of the contemporary relevance of English groups such as the Lollards and Diggers, both of whom have some Anabaptist themes, now be called for?

• *Disembodied Anabaptism*. British Anabaptists can at times rejoice that they, unlike the Bruderhof or North American Mennonites, have not sullied their ideals with the compromises of institutional existence. The "home" which the "new Anabaptists" construct can thus be artificial and even unreal. There are problems with this. Anabaptists, from the sixteenth century onwards, have always been intensely concerned with the practice of discipleship and the experience of community; and they might well be somewhat impatient with an Anabaptism that serves as an ideal which enables a critique of all religious traditions. They might also wonder whether Anabaptism as an unembodied "ideal" can survive across the generations. If Anabaptist or "hyphenated-Anabaptist" groups do not develop in Britain, might Anabaptism simply prove to have been a rather eccentric fad of the 1990s?

• *New ways of being church*. A renewed interest in church planting in the British Isles is but one indication of fresh thinking about what it means to be church in post-Christendom. There are others: the decline of long-established denominations, the proliferation of ethnic and youth churches, the language of "missionary congregations" and attempts to convert congregations into cell churches. When epithets such as post-modern and post-denominational are added to post-Christendom, the complexity of the environment and the importance of discovering authentic and relevant ways of being church become apparent. Christians from many traditions are asking searching questions about the shape, style and ethos of congregational life. Some of the stories suggest that the Anabaptist tradition, which grew out of a sixteenth-century church planting movement, offers important clues for those searching for new ways of being church. Will this require the planting of "Anabaptist" churches, the "Anabaptising" of existing congregations, or both?

• *Urban Anabaptists*. Another surprising discovery is the number of story writers living in urban contexts and finding Anabaptist insights helpful in urban mission and ministry. The British perception of North American Anabaptism is primarily of Mennonite farmers and barn-raising rural communities. But it is in the inner cities and on housing estates that many "new Anabaptists" are attempting to express the values and live out the principles that they have found in the

Anabaptist story. Will Anabaptism prove to be adaptable enough, rugged enough, engaged enough to flourish in this context and to nurture faithful discipleship? As a marginalised tradition, what can it contribute to communities which are socially and economically marginal and where the church also has for so long been marginal? Perhaps the emergence of new forms of Anabaptist-flavoured church life in urban communities might point the way forward for the church in post-Christendom?

These, then, for Christians on both sides of the Atlantic, are a few points to ponder. There will be many others. For this book is rich in its diversity; the stories come from an amazing range of people – from Roman Catholic to Quaker. As editors, we have been concerned to let the writers tell their stories in their own way, rather than trying to impose uniformity on them. We have reduced the length of some stories, removing sentences or paragraphs, but we have not changed the style or focus of the stories – with one significant exception. We have removed from the stories the names of most of the individuals, including our own names, whom the writers identified as important in their discovery of Anabaptism.

Why have we done this? When we first presented the stories to our publisher, he expressed concern that a few names (especially the names of the book's co-editors) kept cropping up in them. We explained that this was simply the way in which people had told their stories. We commented also that this is how networks develop – people are important links and friendships are crucial. Though sympathetic to these responses, our publisher replied that the repeated names distracted him from the stories and might give the impression that the book was intended to commend the people named. Could the stories be told largely without the names of living persons? We thought carefully about this and consulted the Theological Circle which had originally proposed the collecting of the stories.

Finally, we decided to delete most of the names. We would leave in references to books and writers, institutions and courses; but we would remove the names of those who were personal links in the network's development. This has not been an easy decision, nor one that all the writers will welcome. It may leave the impression that books and institutions have been the dominant influences. But we have heeded the advice of a publisher whom we trust and who is committed as we are to ensuring that the story of the contemporary rediscovery of Anabaptism in the British Isles is told in a way that many will find accessible.

The stories are central. But the second part of the book contains four further contributions, again from a diverse group of people, which set the stories in a wider context. These are:

• a theological reflection on these stories by Professor Christopher Rowland, an Anglican New Testament scholar (whose concluding comments pick up again the issue of significant people in the development of a network);

• an older story – of the Anabaptist cell which was destroyed on Easter Sunday 1575 – told by Alan Kreider, a Mennonite historian and missionary;[1]

• an analysis of the present resurgence of interest in Anabaptism in the British Isles by Stuart Murray, who teaches in a Baptist college and is involved in church planting and urban ministry;[2]

• a call to future faithfulness by Noel Moules, a New Church discipleship trainer and "shalom activist."

We offer these stories and essays to you with joy and in the expectant hope that God can use the witness of Anabaptists – past, present and future – in ways that are greater than we can ask or imagine.

NOTES

[1] This is a revised version of a paper presented at a gathering of representatives of the Anglican and Anabaptist traditions at the London Mennonite Centre in October 1993, the first formal conversations of this kind since the sixteenth century. Excerpts from the four papers presented then are included in *Anabaptism Today* Issue 5 (February 1994):3-12. An earlier version of Alan's paper was published as "Mennonite/ Anabaptist Perceptions of Relationships with the Church of England" in *Crucible* (Jan/Mar 1994):3-17.

[2] This is a revised and updated version of a paper first presented in June 1994 at the Anabaptist Vision conference at Elizabethtown, Pennsylvania and published in the *Conrad Grebel Review* (Winter 1995): 87-96.

PART I

COMING HOME:
THE REDISCOVERY OF A HERITAGE
STORIES OF ANABAPTISTS
IN BRITAIN AND IRELAND

A Different Way of Doing Church
Bob Allaway, Wood Green

Bob Allaway is pastor of the Eldon Road Baptist Church, Wood Green, London.

I came to Christ from outside the church. A scientist by profession, I treated with great scepticism all claims to authority that could not appeal to testable facts. Concerned about suffering and injustice in the world about me, I was of the far left politically, though my scepticism made me suspicious of political parties and ideologies.

An evangelical Christian in my laboratory commanded respect for his beliefs by his Christ-like nature, even if he was a Bible-thumper. Hence, I gave him the courtesy of listening to his arguments, and taking the trouble to seek to refute them. Since he stressed that the entire Christian faith rested on the historicity of Christ's resurrection, I endeavoured to disprove this . . . and failed!

This caused me to read the New Testament with an open mind. I slowly surrendered my life to Christ's Lordship, as I became aware of my sin before God, and his overwhelming grace to me in Christ. I believed I should be baptised into membership of a church, and the Baptists seemed most scriptural (and agreeable to my politics!) with their believers' baptism and egalitarian form of church government. The first time I attended, I saw a fellow Christian student had brought a tramp to church with him. This is the place for me, I thought.

Having intended to be theologically liberal, I found such theology was not true to my own experience of God's sovereignty and grace in Christ. In writings of the Reformers and Puritans, I felt really at home. Yet I was frustrated to find that the Reformers did not seem to follow their own theology through to what I took to be its logical conclusion, in a Baptist pattern of church, and egalitarian politics and social concern. Then I became aware of the Radical Reformation, and those who had dared to follow Christ, as they read of him in the Gospels, wherever he might lead them.

In the historical Anabaptists, I catch a vision of a different way of doing church: not entering something static, but joining a group of people travelling after Jesus (even if they are not sure where he is leading them), who, in following him, are made like him (which is where I came in, see above). Since my call to pastoral ministry, I have sought to serve churches in predominantly working-class areas. These are the areas on which the mainstream churches are failing to have much impact. Anabaptism, at its start, was a movement that won to Christ multitudes of ordinary working people.

I will give one example of how Anabaptism has impacted my life. In *Anabaptism Today* 2 (February 1993) there is an article on Hubmaier's Communion Service. I was particularly struck by the use of the Pledge of Love. Shortly thereafter, I was asked to speak at a local Baptist ministers' fraternal. I conducted a Hubmaier style Communion, explaining the theology behind it in the sermon. My fellow ministers responded positively, so I proposed to my then church that we should introduce a Pledge of Love into our Communion service. They refused, but only after serious discussion, in which there was much soul-searching as to the meaning of baptismal vows and church membership, as well as communion.

Shortly after being called to my present church, I was asked to have a midweek communion for the church in Holy Week. Since something special was expected, and the church had shared my vision in calling me, I gave them an Anabaptist Communion, with updated Pledge of Love (I used examples such as Dirk Willems [*Anabaptism Today* 6] to illustrate what this meant in practice). This made a deep impression on all present, so much so that one telephoned a member who was away on holiday, just to tell him about it.

Getting a Little Nearer to New Testament Church Life
Stanley J. Baker, Cardiff

Stanley Baker has been involved for almost fifty years in either pastoral or interdenominational ministries.

I was converted to Christ as a teenager. In my early twenties it dawned on me that the denominational church to which I then belonged was in many respects unlike the New Testament Church. Since then I have spent my whole life searching for the form of church life that is nearest to New Testament Christianity. I am now seventy-five years of age; active, but not in perfect health.

During the years I have worked for interdenominational Christian societies and been pastor of two church congregations. One was an Evangelical Free Church, the other run very much on the lines of a Brethren Assembly. Always I have felt that it would be possible to get a little nearer to New Testament church life.

It was in the 1970s, when I read, *The Reformers and their Stepchildren,* by Leonard Verduin, that I felt that the early Anabaptists had made a real attempt to recover the life and worship of the early church. It was this that stimulated my interest.

I appreciate that I have a lot more to learn. My contacts with the people interested in Anabaptism have been few. However, the copies of *Anabaptism Today* and books from the Metanoia Book Service have helped to enlarge my understanding.

Experiencing the Threat of New Wine
Simon Barrow, Brighton

Simon Barrow is Associate Secretary of the Churches' Commission on Mission at Churches Together in Britain and Ireland

When I heard news of the first official talks between Mennonite and Roman Catholic theologians in Autumn 1998, something important stirred within me. Although my own spiritual formation has taken place principally within Anglicanism, I have also been shaped powerfully by the impulses of Anabaptism and Catholicism – though in ways conforming neither to Rome nor to Lancaster County, nor (for that matter) to Canterbury.

No, for me a church which is truly the Body of Christ and which conveys really Good News to the world has to be characterised by something more Spirit-driven than just the recovered traditions of the past or organised church life, important though those are. Instead, it requires a fresh synthesis of radical catholicity and radical reformation. I shall try to explain why.

My upbringing was determinedly evangelical, tempered with kindly humanitarianism. In my late teens, I found myself catapulted into political campaigning by a passionate sense of the injustices of the world. Yet this stance was frequently at odds with the conservatism of my church and went unnourished by its largely individualistic theological ethos. My decision to study at the London Bible College in the late 1970s was an attempt to bridge these gaps. It didn't work. The more I immersed myself in evangelicalism, the less adequate its assumptions, theories and practices seemed for the world I inhabited. But the one person who impressed me was the Mennonite then teaching church history.

This was only the beginning of my encounter with Anabaptism. Early attempts to tackle political concerns through faith (a small network called *Christians for Justice in Development*, launched in 1980) brought me into contact with the London Mennonite Centre.

It was a fruitful, though not always easy relationship. My growing understanding of justice and peace as central features of the gospel was nurtured by Mennonite spirituality. But my inner-city experience made me uneasy with the world-rejecting elements of Mennonite ecclesiology.

Meanwhile, the world moved on. Thatcherism aided the crisis of the left – where my practical commitments lay. The mid-1980s shock waves destabilised not just my over-optimistic socialist outlook but my cosy Christian orthodoxy too. It was not so much a loss of faith as the beginning of its reconstruction. My Anabaptist instincts made me ask much harder questions about the significance of the church as alternative community. The difficulty was in finding actual expressions of church that cared for counter-cultural values, especially economic ones.

Through the catholic influences on many of my mentors I began slowly to understand that one could be held by "transcendence-in-the-midst" even while failing to grasp it intellectually. Here was the dim dawning of a sacramental sensibility overtaking enthusiasm and rationalism. Overt Anabaptist influences on my faith journey were now few. But at the end of my time in Southwark, I met, and later married, Carla Roth. From a large Mennonite family, Carla's journey had led her to the Episcopal Church. We had developed similar Anabaptist-influenced catholic leanings, and were now fellow dissidents within Anglicanism.

I became convinced that a Christianity which can evoke radical biblical faith without absolutising its own sources or traditions is both vital and possible. But my experience of British Anabaptism is that it is too cocooned to perceive the need for such risky theological creativity. Being tiny and footloose, it has not yet had to face the full force of fragmentation which has eroded established Christian denominations. It is able, rightly, to critique their Christendom assumptions – but perhaps too easily. Yet if it continues to reject the adaptations to late capitalist culture which have helped other evangelical groups to grow, Anabaptism will also need to evolve.

So what are the sources of renewal? One of mine is the robust peace church tradition. Anabaptism understands that violence is the very fabric of evil and the cross of Christ is its polar opposite – the absorption of death, rooted in an unshakeable faith in the ultimate triumph (resurrection) of a love that has the divine capacity to endure suffering for the sake of right.

A church which truly lives this faith, will inevitably be counter-cultural and minority-oriented, living in tension with the state, as Anabaptists have long understood – and as we Anglicans must learn. And it will be rooted in orthopraxis – the restless, neighbour-loving search for Christ-like shalom, rather than for the rationalist certainties of enforced orthodoxy.

But there is a problem. For my experience is that Anabaptism can, at the same time, be world-denying (non-resistant, quietest, self-centring), theologically ineffectual (naively biblicist, unable to embrace plurality, locked in pre-critical thought categories) and exclusive (seeing salvation as the extrication of Christians alone from a doomed world). The universal *evangel* made visible for us in Christ can be trapped in a narrow ideology. This is my temptation too.

As a parallel to some Anabaptist pietism, my catholic eucharistic tradition can also shrink into mere routine. It can colonise the world instead of freeing it, and its theology can become magisterial legitimation rather than the revisionary, contextual, renewable and provisional source of communal discovery and correction it could be. This is why I believe it needs renewing through the spirit of radical reformation.

So I find myself thoroughly in debt to Anabaptism. Yet I am seeking to apply its gifts through a socialistic, ecumenical Anglican catholicism which, in its theological approach, universalist intentions and liturgical symbolism, is deeply problematic for some particularist, anti-ritualist Anabaptists! It remains my vision – that radical reformation and radical catholicity belong together. But this is only possible in the spirit of Jesus' terrifying warning to us all about new wineskins for new wine.

A Close Encounter with Anabaptism
Eoin de Bhaldraithe, O.Cist., Moone, Ireland

Brother Eoin de Bhaldraithe is Prior of Bolton Abbey, Moone, Co. Kildare, Ireland.

I was born in 1938 in the strongly Catholic environment of the West of Ireland. We used to boast that in our parish there was no public house, policeman or Protestant! It was only when I came to live in County Kildare some twenty-five years later that I first encountered Protestants socially.

In 1970, however, I met a Protestant of a different type. Tony Coffey was an Irish Catholic who had become a member of the Church of Christ as he was seeking a community based on the Scriptures and which would never change from that. He came to visit me over a number of months insisting that, according to the New Testament, faith comes before baptism. I had been baptised first and my faith only came later. He said that, to be genuine, I should be baptised again (anabaptised!) and leave the Catholic Church. I had no intention of leaving, but the episode certainly introduced me to Anabaptism. I did say to him that I would keep it in mind and look at it in my research. If I became convinced, the authentic road for me would be to urge the Catholic Church to accept the genuine way.

During those years, as I watched the painful progress of the Irish conflict, I tended to become pacifist. It seemed to be the only realistic response to the teachings of Jesus.

In 1979 the newly elected Pope John Paul II came to Ireland. He took what I thought was a strongly pacifist line by comparison with what the local Catholic bishops were saying. In my commentary on his speeches, I used the book, *The Politics of Jesus*, by John Howard Yoder as a kind of control. Here was a genuine pacifist, and how did the Pope compare?

When the article was published, I sent a copy to Yoder, who wrote to a newly formed group of Mennonites living in Dublin inviting them to contact me. This led to a most fruitful acquaintance with a historic Anabaptist church. I recorded my excitement at the discovery of an article in 1987 on Michael Sattler. A Benedictine, like myself, he left his Black Forest monastery in 1525, was anabaptised, and produced the *Schleitheim Confession*, perhaps the main Anabaptist document.

Today the Pope rules out almost all war as unjust. If we kill in self-defence, he says, we must do it in love. Though this sounds silly, it is a clear echo of Augustine. Apparently he feels that this is as far back as he can go.

One becomes more and more convinced nowadays that baptism was originally for adults only. The work of patristics scholar Everett Ferguson (Church of Christ) shows how clinical baptism came in for children who were dying. Eventually this was generalised for all infants. One ought to have a healthy scepticism about the results of research. If, however, these conclusions are genuine they call the Roman Catholic Church back to the original pacifism and to a faith that precedes initiation.

An Anabaptist from Constantine's Garrison
Jonathan Blakeborough, York

Jonathan Blakeborough is a psychiatrist working in Ilkley and a member of the Acomb Christian Fellowship.

My wife and I grew up, and continue to live, in the city of York. York was founded as a military garrison by the Romans in AD 71, the city where Constantine was proclaimed Tetrarch as a prelude to becoming Christendom's first emperor, notorious among the Jews as the site of England's worst medieval pogrom, and a city that remains host to both the British Army's N.E. Command and the northern primate of the Established Church. Nevertheless, it also has a strong Quaker tradition and is perhaps not quite so inauspicious a place in which to be a peace church Christian.

I am also an Anglican by origin. Bedtime prayers with my mother, Sunday school, Cub Scouts, singing in the church choir and evangelistic summer camps, during one of which I committed my life to the Lord, were the major features of the landscape of my childhood and early adolescence.

To some it may seem a little fanciful to try to make too strong a connection between scouting and the military, except to note that both are uniformed organisations. However, as a youngster, I have to confess that I found all uniforms and their paraphernalia utterly fascinating, and by the age of eighteen I was visiting army bases as a candidate for officer training.

Nevertheless, all was to change on a memorably cloudless afternoon during my final school holidays. As a "potential officer," I was part of an Anglo-West German patrol collecting routine information along the border of the now defunct DDR. Having walked through a village literally cut in half by electric fences and razor wire, we came across a place in open country where a section of the Iron Curtain had been taken down for repairs! Teenage conscripts were digging holes for new fence posts, but nearby were heavily-armed sentries to prevent anyone defecting. It occurred to me that if one of the Easterners decided to make a run for it across no man's land, it would take only a few seconds for the shooting to start. All of us, West and East, would be caught out in the open, so it would not be our weapons that would keep us alive, but everyone's restraint – now there's a thought!! I wasn't afraid, but on that beautiful July day felt profoundly shabby, an apprentice to a dirty trade. It was the beginning of the end of my military career.

Years later, as medical students, my wife and I decided to broaden our ecclesiastical horizons and began to attend a Baptist church. Like many before us, we opted to be "rebaptised" as believers, but subsequently seldom came across other Christians who combined Baptist-style beliefs (believers' baptism, separation of church and state, and priesthood of all believers) with a radical social vision and non-violence, until a theological friend suggested that I get in contact with the London Mennonite Centre, who in turn put me in touch with the nascent Anabaptist Network. At long last, I could put a name to what I had become, an Anabaptist from Constantine's garrison. Maybe now is the time for me to recruit a few more and establish an outpost of the Prince of Peace.

Unsettling in a Disturbing and yet Glorious Way
Andrew Bolton, Leicester

Andrew Bolton is an Englishman who recently moved to Independence, Missouri, to be Peace and Justice Ministries Coordinator at the international headquarters of the Reorganized Church of Latter Day Saints.

I remember being intrigued by a *Sunday Times* article about the Amish. At that time I was training to do something about hunger agriculturally – by doing a degree in plant sciences. A further indirect push was reading Ron Sider's *Rich Christians in an Age of Hunger* and *Christ and Violence*. *Rich Christians in an Age of Hunger* was a particularly important book for me in the late 1970s and early 1980s. I was beginning to understand that hunger would not end by just technological or scientific innovation. Hunger, I was discovering, was caused by colonialism, economic systems, kinds of cultures and poverty of vision and spirit. To read a radically biblical perspective on wealth and poverty in the contemporary world was very exciting. However, it was when I was doing a course on the history of Christian thought for an MA degree in 1984-85 that I really discovered Anabaptism. I was so struck by the sixteenth-century Anabaptists that I persuaded my teacher to let me do two essays rather than just one on the Anabaptists. I was in the USA at the time but not located near any Mennonites. However, when I came back with my family to the UK, we went to visit the Mennonite Centre in London and met Alan Kreider. Subsequently, I came across the Hutterites through visits and then a year-long stay at the Darvell Bruderhof in Robertsbridge, East Sussex.

It is important at this point to explain that I am a member of the RLDS church – the Reorganised Church of Jesus Christ of Latter Day Saints. I had been attracted to this movement by the quality of people I met when living in Germany for a year just after I had graduated. Ordinary Germans on the whole treated me as a second-class citizen. I spoke bad German and I was a foreigner and I understood why I was looked down on. Unfortunately the English do exactly the same to foreigners. However, the German RLDS church members treated me as first class: I was a human and welcomed and loved. They also had this dream of the kingdom of God on earth, which they called Zion, an expression of the Acts 2 community in Jerusalem being lived out today. The early members of the church had tried to live this out.

The RLDS Church is frequently confused with the Mormons – The Church of Jesus Christ of Latter-day Saints. It is true that we share some things in common – the first fourteen years of history from 1830-1844, the Book of Mormon, and belief in revelation through contemporary prophets. However, the Anabaptist experience of Münster, North Germany in 1533-1535 is paralleled by the Latter Day Saint experience of Nauvoo, Illinois in 1839-1844. The Mormons are an unrepentant continuation of what happened in Nauvoo. Members of the RLDS Church rejected Nauvoo and could be argued to be a sort of "Mennonite" equivalent.

I have been very grateful for the influence of the RLDS Church: its fellowship, hopes, teachings and witness of Jesus have really blessed my life. However, looking at Anabaptism helps me see the very best in my own tradition even more clearly. It helps me further clarify what it means to be a disciple of Jesus and seeker of the kingdom of God. Let me give some examples: the ongoing work of the Holy Spirit, believers' baptism and communion as ordinances, the importance of an implicit theology of discipleship, the Gospels and the Sermon on the Mount as the canon within the canon, non-violence, priesthood of all believers, stewardship, mutual help, and community. I am encouraged and uplifted by the example of both sixteenth-century Anabaptists and twentieth-century Anabaptists. Dialogue with contemporary Anabaptism and its sixteenth-century roots helps me sort out the gospel more clearly.

At this point in its history the RLDS Church is seeking to discover what it means to be a people "dedicated to the pursuit of peace." Anabaptism can help us. But it has also unsettled me in a disturbing and yet glorious way. On the one hand, the witness of Anabaptism points to a way of salvation that can help us out of the difficulties of war, violence, marital unfaithfulness and greed that plague our post-modern world. On other hand, there is the high cost of discipleship.

I Seek a Way of Living
Kevin G. Brown, Hackney

Kevin Brown is pastor of the Downs Baptist Church, Hackney.

My own encounter with the Anabaptists occurred some five years ago on entering Northern Baptist College for training as a minister. I joined the Anabaptist Study Group. Within weeks I had been captivated by the visionary message of the early Anabaptist pioneers, and I eagerly awaited the fortnightly gatherings around the tea and biccies to plunder the treasury of these wonderful sixteenth-century mystics, coveting their communities and recognising my own shortcomings.

However, it was not the academic enquiry that really drew my attention. Certainly it tickled my intellectual fancy to discover a radical biblical alternative to the doubt-laden liberal theology of much of university life. But I believe my fascination grew out of seeing two Mennonite believers living out much of what we shared as students in discussion. I was drawn by their practice of peacemaking and longed to be able to share my vision of God and his kingdom in the loving way they did. I wanted to be part of a community that lived and breathed and had their being like these folk did.

Today, as an inner-city church leader, what I seek is a way of living in and from the principles of New Testament life, which so gripped the Anabaptists throughout the centuries. Too much Christian practice can be summed up as merely reflecting on how savoury the salt was, and how bountiful the light. The very essence of our faith is that what we have must be shared. This was the message of the post-Pentecost Christian community, which "enjoyed the favour of all the people" (Acts 2.47). This was the force of the people who came and turned the world upside down.

My own turbulent history as a believer is in part due to the poor heritage of discipleship to which I have fallen victim during my Christian life. Where then do we go for an alternative? I believe to the counter-cultural dynamic of the New Testament community, and to the very same stories which motivated the Anabaptists to take God at his word. For these people issues of state, the taking of oaths and arms were the issues of the day. Much of this remains true, but we need too to recognise the need for the Church to take the lead on matters of sexuality, race, democratic politics, community, economics and kingdom-living in a fractured and hopeless world.

Inner cities are full of very lonely people. They more than ever before need to know that someone does care enough to greet them, help them, pray for them and be there for them. If that does not represent a mission opportunity, then what does? What the Anabaptists have left me with is a desire to find answers to such questions in the context of the believing community. Jesus said little children were precious. In a world that abuses them we have to ask if they have ceased to be those who know what the kingdom is like. Do we really wrestle against flesh and blood, or does the Christian community have something more to offer? Has there ever been a time where peacemaking and truth-telling have been more needed? These are aspects of Anabaptist heritage which the Church itself needs to hear and to learn, never mind the wider community. These are the inescapable realities that the voices of the Anabaptists call out to me about through history and through the reality of today's world. Who am I to ignore their cries?

The Anglican Vicar's Tale
Chris Burch, Coventry

Canon Christopher Burch is Precentor of Coventry Cathedral.

In 1982 I became vicar of St. Agnes', a parish in inner city Leeds. It had attracted a small group of intellectual evangelicals from outside the parish boundary, who were actively seeking to link their spirituality with issues of social justice, both locally and internationally (every inner-city vicar should have such a group!). They had formed a city-wide inter-church group called the *Aslan Education Unit.*

In 1983, two Mennonites came to Leeds to speak at a day conference run by the Unit, called "It all fits together." Spirituality and social justice, loving God and loving your neighbour, raising hands in triumph and weeping at the sin of Jerusalem (or Leeds) – it was the first time I heard speakers bring them all together in a satisfying way, though I had long felt instinctively that they must belong together. Over the years we enjoyed a deep, if irregular, contact with them. For me the fact that they were Anabaptists mattered less than the insight they brought to us (e.g. when they preached together at St. Agnes').

I don't know how much they influenced the ministry at St Agnes' – we were influenced also by the Community of Celebration, not least in its positive attitude to work with children – but I do know that, by the time we had to work on a disagreement over the Remembrance Sunday service, between pacifists in the congregation and the British Legion, I was conscious of being under Anabaptist influence. The process of negotiation at that time was more important for me than the outcome: I would never have thought of that unaided!

In 1993, I was invited out of the blue to attend a symposium of Anglicans and Anabaptists in London: the first official dialogue since the sixteenth century, when the outcome had been fatal for the Anabaptists. I was overwhelmed by the strength of the sense of history, the living memory of persecution of Anabaptists, and the depth of feeling which it still engendered. I began to think of the Anabaptist story as worth getting to know, where previously I had regarded it as a bit irrelevant.

I spent the first half of the 1990s researching and writing a thesis on spirituality in the inner city, in which Anabaptist ideas played an important part. This was helped by my supervisor, who has done a good deal to widen the influence of Anabaptist thought in academic theology. I was attracted by the concept (though not all the outworkings) of the narrative theologians, and was not altogether surprised to discover their links with Anabaptists in the USA. At the same time, St. Agnes' was trying to work out the meaning of its new status as a local ecumenical project, with Anglican and Baptist membership. The sacrament of baptism was no problem, but our very different ecclesiologies were more difficult to handle!

Then, in 1995, I became Canon Precentor of Coventry Cathedral. They knew what they were getting, because I had mentioned Anabaptist ideas in my application. Cathedrals are by definition big institutions, and they have to relate (positively or negatively) with other big institutions, not least those of local and national government. We entertain infantry regiments to cathedral services – though we do insist they leave their guns outside. We also pursue an international ministry of peace and reconciliation, and I was privileged to be a small part of that, on trips to Romania in 1996 and to South Africa in 1997. The Truth and Reconciliation Commission in South Africa is, I believe, a creative breakthrough in human history – inspired by that definitive breakthrough achieved by Jesus Christ.

I now attend the twice-yearly conferences of the Anabaptist Theological Network, where I have the job of saying "so what?!" whenever our feet get detached from the ground! I remain an Anglican by conviction, and realise that neither my beliefs nor my position would enable me to become a signed-up Anabaptist. But I am also convinced that Anabaptist ideas, and the Anabaptist story, are an important part of the Christian inheritance of the whole Church. Among other things, they remind us of our need to repent of aspects of our own history, and of the possibilities of living as Christian communities without the secular privileges we have enjoyed for so long. These may be crucial to the readjustment that the Church will have to go through if our present society becomes unstable or unsustainable.

A Foil to Judge my Actions and Political Theology
David Campanale, London

David Campanale is a television news producer for BBC's international channel, BBC World; has served as a local government councillor, has been Vice-Chair of the Movement for Christian Democracy, and is a member of the Community Church, Chessington.

In 1982, and a few years after becoming a Christian, I chose to be baptised by immersion as a response to what I sensed to be the plain reading of the New Testament. This was how I was introduced to the term "Anabaptist." In my local Anglican church, where I had worshipped since childhood, I was advised that to be baptised "twice" (they only recognised the validity of my infant christening) meant that I could no longer claim to be Anglican. The vicar's wife explained I was now an "Anabaptist." And here began a search for the story of Anabaptism.

In the first instance I joined one of the new house churches, where I was introduced to ideas of the priesthood of all believers; the use of spiritual gifts for the benefit of the body of Christ; plurality of leaders, including women; and the involvement of everyone (including children) in the worship, prayer, sharing of the eucharist and in most aspects of the life of the church.

A Christian who had introduced me to the new church scene also had an interest in Anabaptism. We travelled to visit the Hutterites at the Darvell Bruderhof in Robertsbridge, Sussex, and began a friendship that continues to this day. Their publication, *The Plough*, has been the strongest influence on me from an Anabaptist perspective. The historical roots of the movement in central Europe also meant my path crossed with another part of the family – the Mennonites – during the transition period to democracy in the former Warsaw Pact countries. I travelled to the USA and went to visit Mennonite churches in Kansas and elsewhere. So, as well as being influenced by the theological ideas in Anabaptism, I tried to get an insight into how these affected both "old style" Anabaptist communities (the Hutterites) and how modern-day Anabaptists have developed (the Mennonites, for example – though the story is more complicated).

At present, as someone committed to serving God in politics, the Anabaptist perspective has become one "foil" against which I judge my actions and political theology. In particular, the place of the Cross in the struggle against the Powers.

A New Approach to Interpersonal Conflict
Joe Campbell, Belfast

Joe Campbell is Assistant Director of the Mediation Network, Belfast, and an elder in a Presbyterian church in Holywood.

A Presbyterian from birth who is now an elder in my local congregation, I first encountered the Mennonites in casual conversation in 1980 with a colleague who was working with youth on urban justice issues in England and had visited the London Mennonite Centre. He spoke of a quality of community life, worship where justice and peace issues were not on the edge but central, and a people who took Jesus' call to be peacemakers as a serious call for today. To say I was interested would be an understatement. I read John Howard Yoder's *Politics of Jesus* and I knew then I had to learn more about this church.

At this point in my life I was Youth Director of Belfast YMCA, a protestant and evangelical youth organisation. I was responsible for running a social education and recreation programme for several hundred youth (16-25 age group), mostly from low income inner-city backgrounds and a healthy mix of male and female, Catholic and Protestant. Those young people who had regular jobs were the exception as the young people often came from neighbourhoods where over seventy per cent of the people were on welfare. Few experiences in my life had prepared me for the hopeless injustice faced by those youth. I understood in stark terms the connection between social deprivation and political violence. Many of the young people I worked with had lives outside the YMCA in the junior ranks of paramilitary organisations on both sides of our divided society.

The other element for me in my work in the Y was getting to work alongside Catholics who took faith seriously. Schools then and largely now were either Catholic or Protestant. Mine was Protestant with only Protestant teachers. My training as an engineer in the Belfast shipyard brought only occasional contact with Catholics in its almost exclusively Protestant workforce. I had been raised in a divided extended family. My grandfather, a Protestant, being brave enough at the turn of the century to marry a Catholic woman, have eleven children and raise them male Catholic, female Protestant. This unique family history has given to me a sensitivity to and awareness of both sides in our divided society, something at this end of the century I am eternally grateful for.

These twin issues of working for justice, and growing awareness of faithful Catholics wanting to walk with God as I did was the seedbed in which my growing interest in the Mennonite church took root.

In 1987, with support from Mennonite institutions, my wife Janet and I and our three children had a ten-month sabbatical in the USA, living and studying at a Mennonite seminary. Attending classes, reading in the excellent library and being part of a Mennonite congregation and small group was refreshing and energising. I gained valuable theological underpinning for justice and peace work. I came to understand the Mennonite story. We experienced church as community with God's people responsible to and for one another. I was under no pressure to become a Mennonite or indeed even to attend a Mennonite congregation, and our Presbyterian tradition was never devalued. I trained as a victim offender mediator, completed six cases and undertook further training with the Mennonite Conciliation Service

Ron Kraybill was one of a number of Mennonite Church workers who came to Belfast for short visits. Ron ran a three-hour workshop on conflict skills and mediation for my team of YMCA youth workers. That evening lives with me still as I remember what then was a new approach to interpersonal conflict. It was biblically based and practical. I was energised and hungry for more. In addition to running another two-day workshop on mediation in Dublin, Ron ran a session at the Corrymeela Reconciliation Centre and presented them with a Mennonite Central Committee Peace Library. But it was those first short workshops on conflict and mediation that were to sow the seeds among a diverse group of grassroots community workers and peace activists that led in 1990 to the founding of Mediation Network in Belfast. Now I find myself its Assistant Director. We have eight staff and are involved in a wide range of peace-building activity in Northern Ireland, from political dialogue, community mediation and training, working with police on issues of culture, ethos and community policing, through to other public sector and community organisations and churches, helping them to respond to conflict in ways which enable relationships to be built and conflict to be transformed.

Christians Can Offer New Ways Ahead
David Cockburn, Bradford

David Cockburn is doing an MA in Peace Studies in the University of Bradford and is hoping to work in peacemaking, from a Christian standpoint.

I first became aware of historical Anabaptists while doing a Christian leadership and discipleship course called *Workshop* in 1990-1991. I did not discover more for a while, but there were a number of interesting books on the bookstall written by Mennonites or Anabaptists!

After reading Physics in 1976-79, I worked for the defence electronics business of EMI. I several times worked through the "Christians in defence" debate, and was reasonably happy with the job. The crucial question seemed to me to be that if I believed in military defence for my country, but was not prepared to work in it, then I would be getting other people to do my dirty work for me!

In 1990-93 I was working in Germany. Visiting Munich, I went to Dachau, a concentration camp set up in 1933 for Jews, homosexuals, gypsies, communists, and common criminals. This had a profound effect on me, in particular that many of the locals knew about the camp, and what happened there, but were unwilling or unable to do anything about it. This visit created in me a desire not to let such things happen again, if I could do anything about it. The Yugoslavian crisis was beginning, and I felt very powerless – I did not know how to understand the situation, let alone interact with it for change. Then the Rwanda genocide occurred, and I realised that the world had not learnt how to prevent such atrocities, and also that I did not have any idea of solutions, Christian or otherwise.

Just after the start of the first IRA ceasefire, a member of the Mediation Network in Belfast came to London to talk at the London Mennonite Centre. His talk, spirituality, style, and indication of ways of working towards helping to resolve the conflict opened my eyes to new possibilities. The atmosphere at the centre was strangely like "coming home." I was invited to an Anabaptist Network Study Group, and over the next couple of years found it to be refreshingly different to my Church. I had never been in a "peace church," and found the peace agenda attractive but challenging, with people of deep spirituality and peace. The history of the Anabaptists seemed to give pointers to old ways of living which were also very new, radical, and practical alternatives. Over the next couple of years, I attended courses led by Mennonites on conflict resolution, finding new ways to resolve old problems, and an awareness of God being very much a peacemaker.

Life at the time was also changing dramatically at work. In common with many people, work had become more pressurised and less supporting to individuals. Some difficult changes led me to start reconsidering whether I should be in defence work, and when in March 1997 I was unexpectedly offered a very good position within the company, realising that it would tie me into another three to four years of hassle, I turned it down on the grounds that I was getting out of defence work in the next six to nine months!

The next months were challenging, obtaining a place on the MA course at Bradford, with the chance to look in depth at some of the very difficult questions. The sense of God being involved was exciting, and as I study peace issues I am becoming more convinced that Christians can offer new ways ahead, and of the necessity of prayer – situations are so complex that only God has the wisdom to sort them, but he wants our co-operation.

I have little idea of the future, but feel drawn to working in conflict prevention/post-conflict peace-building, at the national or international level.

A Cutting Edge, just like Jesus
Mike Costello, Sandbach

Mike Costello is a Baptist pastor in Sandbach, Cheshire.

I came to know Jesus in what might be called a localised revival; in fact about half of our street were saved in six months. We were seeing many dynamic conversions and we started to meet together in each other's homes as well as attending the services at the local Baptist church. These home meetings often (at least once a week) turned into all-night prayer and worship meetings; we also met often and shared meals and babysitting, etc. The sense of community was very strong, and to us as new Christians this was the norm.

As I began the journey of theological training at Spurgeon's College, I came into contact with the folks at the London Mennonite Centre and visited a couple of times. What I learned and saw there – coupled with my deep-down belief that the idea of Church as community was fundamental to a right understanding of what Church was all about – led me to look for more. My reformation studies added to this longing for a more realistic expression of Church. Many years later, while pastoring in the Thames valley, I heard of study groups and joined the Home Counties group which was such a blessing. Since moving north, however, I have not as yet found a group that is relatively local.

What has been attractive and helpful to me is this twinning of my spirit and Anabaptist thinking regarding Church as corporate, or community – the emphasis on a family looking to take Scripture as a life guide, to be experienced rather than just read and talked about. Radical discipleship must come to the Church, especially when we take a good look at the way society is today and where we can see it is heading. So many of our expressions of Church, even evangelical and/or charismatic ones, have little or nothing to say to the world around us. Anabaptism had a profound cutting edge, just like Jesus and his early followers. We can only be this kind of disciple together with others (if that makes sense).

How has it impacted my life? More than anything, it is in my function as a leader in a local church. It has helped keep alive the early vision and motivation to see the local church becoming or growing into an effective Christian community. No matter what setbacks and disappointments come (and many do), I have this picture which never goes away. Church from an Anabaptist perspective is such a powerful concept and word. Hopefully it will become a present reality too. I love Jesus' words: "keep on asking, keep on seeking, keep on knocking." Anabaptism helps me to do this.

The Metaphor of Journey is more Helpful than that of Warfare
Trisha Dale, Farnborough

Trisha Dale is a freelance editor, and subscription secretary of the Anabaptist Network.

I was brought up in a nominally Christian home, was christened at the age of eleven, and converted in the evangelical Sunday school of a liberal Anglican church at the age of thirteen. As a sixth-form Christian in the 1960s, I attended Bible studies and sermons given by someone who used an Anabaptist – Jesus-centred – approach to a vigorous exposition of biblical texts. I didn't consciously hear the adjective "Anabaptist" until, having heard that I had by then been baptised as a believer by immersion while at university, the Anglican vicar I asked to conduct my wedding enquired if I wished to be married twice, "You and your Anabaptist principles!" I had to find out what he was getting at!

In the 1980s I attended a Baptist Mainstream conference where, in a session entitled "Social Holiness," I heard a Bible-based argument for recognising God as the provider and protector, and for rejecting nuclear weapons. I had never before heard arguments against nuclear weapons presented from Scripture. In my heart I had had an agreement with the Lord that, if Christians who argued from the Bible that using nuclear weapons was OK with God were correct, then at that point I did not agree with the Bible. This was a very painful tension for me. The exposition gave wonderful affirmation to my gut feeling, and a way of countering the prevailing view while also using the Bible. I've been discovering Anabaptism – its history, people and creative theology – ever since.

Anabaptism offers me a Jesus-centred theology, and a way of living in a Christian body that is constantly open to renewal. It is not full of fixed answers and theological statements. Paradoxically, it is a tradition of no great tradition. The metaphor of journey is more helpful to me than that of warfare and is more prominent in the thinking and practice of my Anabaptist friends. I particularly value the holistic lifestyle with no rigid demarcation between spiritual and sacred.

It's hard to say precisely how Anabaptism has impacted my life. A Jesus-centred approach has sustained me through my investigation of feminism and the Church, and most especially through the traumas of separation and divorce. Over the past four years I have to some extent sought to disentangle the threads of my faith from the strands in my life coming from my background, my marriage, the expectations of others, and the Baptist and Anglican churches in which I have spent many years. Articles in *Anabaptism Today* have reassured me that I am not alone or completely "off the rails" in my thinking and vision, at times when I have been struggling with what I understand some other Christians to believe. And it has given me some wonderful friends!

The Coming Together of a Strong New "Coalition"
Roger Dowley, Swindon

Roger Dowley is retired after many years as a solicitor in East London; he continues his active interest in the life and mission of the urban Church.

My awareness of Anabaptism has always been one element in a broader package of radical nonconformist discipleship. For at least five generations back my ancestors were "Independent Calvinists," practising believers' baptism, and from boyhood I was always "on the side of" the radical "Stepchildren of the Reformation" of the Anabaptist mould.

Along with this went an ingrained regard for Scripture, which looked for meaningful expressions of its challenging standards and lifestyle, and a built-in resistance to contrived and unconvincing rationalisations designed to dilute its challenges. I recall, when I was about twelve, asking why the view of poverty and wealth presented by the Church ran counter to that presented throughout the Bible (and getting no satisfying answer). It was this kind of incongruity that led to my settling in Tower Hamlets in 1938, soon after I qualified as a solicitor.

Specific contact with Anabaptism consisted of reading John Howard Yoder's *Politics of Jesus* and similar writings, and some links with the London Mennonite Centre, but my main involvement has been with urban mission (particularly through the Evangelical Urban Training Project and the Evangelical Coalition for Urban Mission) and will continue to be so until the Church is at least as strong among the disadvantaged as it is in areas of sufficiency.

The record of the faithful witness of the past must be kept fresh before us, but for me the main focus today is the acceleration of the coming together of a strong new "coalition," however loosely structured, incorporating the best insights of the various contemporary biblical groupings which are seeking a better model of church, including Anabaptist emphases among them. At its best, this could signal a New Reformation stretching back beyond the partial Lutheran Reformation and the medieval and Constantinian "great" churches, to the foundational biblical source.

Becoming Better, not Bigger
Richard Eggl, Coleford, Gloucestershire

Richard Eggl is a graduate of religion and history, is married with four children, and works with disabled people as a care-giver, teacher, and foster parent.

I was at school when I first became intrigued by the name "Anabaptist" and promised myself that I would one day find out true details about those Anabaptists. My family background was Lutheran, until my father moved to Gloucestershire for work. The rest of the family followed shortly afterwards and we became "Anglicans."

During my schooldays and later, while on a diocesan training course, I would occasionally uncover a mention of the Anabaptists, but it was not until 1987 in the University of Wales that I delved into reference books in earnest. Towards the end of my undergraduate studies in world religions and history, I chose to study the Mennonites for my thesis. A casual call to Directory Enquiries led to the telephonist surprising me with the number of the

London Mennonite Centre. I had no knowledge, then, of any Mennonite activity in this country.

My faith has been moulded and strengthened by contact with Mennonites. The first change has been the recognition of the need for the separation of the original, New Testament Church from the State. I believe in the separation because the bond that ties an "established" church to the state also binds the same church's confession, thereby restricting the part God wants us to play in his world. This may be a real, but worthwhile challenge to a parent. The aim I have for my family's lifestyle is that we become "better, not bigger," as John Ruth says in his book on the Plain People.

Second, I have noted over a number of years now that there has been a change in the type and character of services in many mainstream churches. Some denominations which in earlier times were refreshingly and vibrantly different in character now share many similarities. The presumed successful recipe (to catch the most people) emerges as a weekly Communion service with ideas borrowed from various sources. Too often, the edification of the soul is not realised. I have enjoyed those Mennonite services I have attended, where simplicity, fellowship and purity in the meetings are important and which ring true when I read the Bible. It is fitting that the Communion service is appropriated to a major occasion, following proper preparation.

Third, I am encouraged by the earlier examples of pacifists and I believe that being a pacifist is the correct way for a Christian to live. Having courage and strength to speak out for what one believes is not always easy, but I believe when it is necessary, ease should not feature.

Finally, I believe fervently in missionary work, to help communities develop or to recover from catastrophes. In an age of rapidly widening gaps between socio-economic groups, I believe, in numerical terms, the Mennonite example of practising missionary and social-help work far exceeds the predictable level for other religious groups, and that this is indicative of a Church that believes.

If my route towards the Mennonites appears to have been mainly academic, I would add only that it is with a genuine desire to follow the teachings of Jesus as closely as possible.

Refocusing our Faith on the Person and Teaching of Jesus

Ben Faulkner, Cradley Heath

Photo not available.

Ben Faulkner is a Family Court welfare officer employed by West Midlands Probation Service and is training as a lay minister (Reader) in the Anglican Church.

I may be wrong (I often am), but I think my first encounter with the term "Anabaptism" was as a teenager watching an episode of *M.A.S.H.*, the funny, but often tragic, American series set during the Korean war. One of the army chaplains, I seem to remember, told a soldier that he was an Anabaptist. A brief discussion with my father, then an Anglican minister, led me to look the term up in one of his reference books. I remember nothing of the contents of this book, but the term "Anabaptism" was seemingly lodged in my memory at that point.

Some ten years later, I came across a letter in the February 1992 edition of the magazine *Third Way*. Under the heading "An Anabaptist Network?" the letter referred to a renewed interest in Anabaptism, mentioning interesting views on the relationship between church and state, radical Jesus-centredness and discipleship. My memory was jolted, and for some reason I wrote for further information. I now find myself helping to run the West Midlands Anabaptist Network study group and on the steering group of the Network. So, what happened?

I began to read the journal with the somewhat unpromising title *Anabaptism Today*. I was impressed and challenged by this group's attempts to take seriously all aspects of the teaching of Jesus, particularly those "difficult bits" which so many church leaders seemed to avoid, or marginalise. Here was a Christian tradition, shaped in community, whose theology and practice was rooted in the experience of persecution and martyrdom for attempting to apply the teaching of Jesus to every part of life. But was this just something from the past, a useful lesson perhaps, but little more?

At the time, I was studying for an MA in social policy and had just begun to work as a probation officer. In the course of my studies, I had become particularly excited by concepts of restorative criminal justice

and victim-offender mediation. I read widely and avidly, convinced
that herein lay the solution to many of the deep-seated problems in
our unwieldy and largely ineffective criminal justice system.

Then, it happened. I suddenly realised that the people who were
pushing back the boundaries of my field of work were the same people
about whom I was reading in *Anabaptism Today*. People with an
Anabaptist heritage were at the forefront of criminal justice reform
today. I became very interested in the connection. I joined a study
group, but had to give this up following my marriage and move to the
West Midlands. There, Barbara and I "did" *Workshop*, a discipleship
and leadership training course which is heavily influenced by
Anabaptist thinking. Following this, we were persuaded to set up a
new Network study group in the West Midlands.

Over the years I have been continually impressed by the integrity
of those within, and attracted to, the Anabaptist tradition. The
historical roots of the tradition give rise to what I believe to be a deep
and rich analysis of both the past and present. The study group here
in the West Midlands has, in my experience, been a place where many
people, from a wide variety of backgrounds, can discuss issues which
are generally not being addressed by their own congregations. In
addition, we eat together and break bread – a powerful symbol in a
society where those from different traditions rarely break bread
together. We also have fun!

So, what of the future? I hope that the Network will continue to act
as a resource for congregations of all denominations, bringing
attention to a group of people who have attempted, and often
succeeded, to refocus their faith on the person and teaching of Jesus.
I do not wish to be party to setting up a new denomination, or group
of fellowships, in this country. I was briefly tempted to believe that I
had found the near-perfect model of being church. However, as with
every other tradition, I soon discovered that historic Anabaptist
congregations have their weaknesses, as well as strengths.

I was not disheartened by this. It confirmed my resolve to remain
within my own Anglican tradition, whose faults I know only too well,
seeking to apply Anabaptist insights to the situations in which I find
myself. May the Network continue to bring new or challenging insights
to the many denominations we already have in this country.

Living as Brothers and Sisters, Sharing the Whole of Life
Derrick and Margaret Faux, Birmingham

Derrick Faux is a retired journalist and printer; Margaret Faux is a retired nursery nurse. Both, in their large house on the outskirts of Birmingham, are tireless hosts of many, including the West Midland Anabaptist Study Group

Our discovery of Anabaptism in 1954 was life-changing and full of surprises! Our conventional way of life was challenged to its roots. Married for two and a half years with two small children, we had been seeking together for some purpose and foundation in our life. Between us we had entered and exited the "Oxford Group," Unitarianism, Quakerism, Bahaism and other movements. However, a casual listening to a soapbox speaker in the Birmingham Bull Ring led us to the Bruderhof, an Anabaptist community living on three adjoining farms in the Clee Hills in Shropshire. We visited for a week and stayed for seven years!

There we found a group of several hundred people, families and singles, sharing their lives and goods in the manner, as they saw it, of the early Christians. They had started in Germany after the First World War, but it was not until some years later that they had discovered Anabaptism among the Hutterians who had taken refuge in North America. The group earnestly studied the early Anabaptist writings and, as a consequence, their way of life became more and more modelled on the sixteenth-century Hutterian communities in Eastern Europe. They believed that Christians had to go beyond personal salvation and live together as brothers and sisters, sharing the whole of life. God, they believed, was calling together his people on the earth.

Our own ideas were shaken. The community life was attractive enough at that stage and we argued that surely it could be lived without the Christian basis. Experience in the first year as guests convinced us that here was something more than a socialist experiment! Our new-found brothers and sisters had found the same spirit of Christ which had led the early Anabaptists not only to devote their lives to one another but to face persecution and even martyrdom, reacting only with love.

Because that was our introduction to Anabaptism, we have found it difficult to separate community from the Christian life. Why we left the Bruderhof is another story, but maintaining our Anabaptist outlook we have gone on seeking fellowship, with an "open house" through which many brothers and sisters have shared our life. Our worship has varied from Quaker meeting, charismatic fellowship and the Anabaptist Network.

We realise that Anabaptism cannot be grasped as a fossil from the past, but must be a lived concept in life today. We must constantly turn to the Bible for inspiration. At the same time, we are encouraged and challenged by the experience of our brothers and sisters in past generations for whom life was very different but who nevertheless devoted themselves to Jesus Christ.

A Charismatic Looking for a Theology – and a Community to Embody It

Tim Foley, London

Tim Foley is an electronics engineer who is on the leadership team of the Wood Green Mennonite Church and is doing the MTh in Baptist and Anabaptist Studies at Spurgeon's College.

Every once in a while I dig out an essay by Tom Smail, in which he relates the cross to the Spirit, and where he questions whether the charismatic renewal is in fact a movement looking for a theology, as some have described it. Looking back over the last few years, I would describe myself as a charismatic who was looking for a theology, found an Anabaptist one, and then had to look for a community who desired to embody that theology. Of course, this helped me to realise the central place of the Church, without which I could not be a disciple, much less an Anabaptist. Recently it has seemed to me that the Anabaptist movement in the UK has itself articulated the same desire for a concrete expression of the Anabaptist vision, for embodiment in community.

The desire for a theology was what led me to enrol at Spurgeon's College almost five years ago, while remaining on the leadership team of a New Church congregation which I had recently helped to plant. It seems to me that when the New Churches were known as House Churches they more clearly embodied aspects of the Anabaptist vision, some of which have now been forgotten. Such vital areas as the ministry of all, anti-clericalism, a practical ecumenism and a commitment to justice were stronger hallmarks then than now.

Stanley Hauerwas once said a student has no mind to make up until his teachers have taught him to have one, and this was certainly my experience with Anabaptism. It truly is a whole new way of looking at things. My first contact with Anabaptism proper was through some of my college teachers. Contrary to the dismissive tone to Anabaptism found in some works of church history, here I had teachers who were positive, even enthusiastic, about the history and impact of the Anabaptist vision. Of course, learning theology can be exciting from many viewpoints, but these teachers helped me to articulate, from an Anabaptist viewpoint, a Christian vision of life through theology, history and the Scriptures. In particular I learned about the importance of the Church, the Church as *polis*, peacemaking, the place of the Old Testament and a Trinitarian theology of the Holy Spirit.

I soon became part of an Anabaptist study group which met at the college. Here I was exposed to hard thinking from an Anabaptist perspective on issues like politics, violence, the charismatic movement and shalom. The atmosphere was quite academic, but as many participants were connected to the college this was not inappropriate (although in many other settings it would have been). I found the stories of early Anabaptism to be almost overwhelming in their portrayal of joyful discipleship and the willingness to die for Christ. Someone said that a theology which marginalised martyrdom was not an interesting theology, and I would like to understand what these stories mean for my church.

I am now privileged to work as a leader in Wood Green Mennonite Church, amongst a people who have struggled to become Anabaptist (and who have grown somewhat tired in the process). The church has so much that I had been looking for, and so in some ways I feel I have reached home. While I don't want to gloss over the real problems which we face as a small congregation, we are doing many things right. The church has a decision-making process in which all members are truly listened to but which is not held up by a small number of members in disagreement. People's gifts are used in leading and planning worship, preaching, small groups, prayer and youth work. It is a challenging place which is not always comfortable but is certainly a community of the Way. We try to be a place where the Jesus Way becomes real and where the Anabaptist vision is embodied.

I Knew I'd Come Home
Roger Forster, Forest Hill, London

Roger Forster, whose wife Faith is also in full-time ministry, is leader of Ichthus Christian Fellowship, a Vice-President of both Tearfund and the Evangelical Alliance.

After I was baptised in the Spirit as a student at Cambridge, about a year after my conversion, I became hungry for something. I was looking around and trying to find my way through the ecclesiastical maze. It was in E.H. Broadbent's book, *The Pilgrim Church*, that I first met the Anabaptists – and I knew the radicals had something to do with my search. That was in the late 1950s. In the 1970s, I read books like George Williams' *The Radical Reformation*, and I knew I'd come home. This was what God had put into my heart when I was searching. It was this kind of church life, community experience, love and non-violence for which I was longing.

Although I didn't know of any Anabaptist communities at the time, I knew historically I had found my roots. My roots were not in the territorial religion of medieval Constantinian days, nor even simply in nonconformity as it had broken away from historic churches. I was looking for something far more radical. I had, as it were, another conversion. I'd come home in my understanding that this was church.

The stories of various Anabaptists became important to me. It was impressive how Michael Sattler stood before accusers, lifting up his hand at execution to show that you can endure the fire. I also found the pilgrimage of Conrad Grebel – his experiences with Zwingli and Felix Manz – very moving. These stories tied up with the kind of spiritual pilgrimage I was on: trying to discover more truth. I also appreciated Balthasar Hubmaier with his intellectual grasp and theological insights. The story and writings of Menno Simons have been inspirational.

With a number of early Anabaptists, such as Sattler and Hubmaier, it appealed to me that their wives were so closely identified with them in their work. They weren't just great male names standing isolated from wife and family, but people whose whole lives were involved in their commitment to Jesus. The Anabaptists were on a long journey that started way behind Luther, but finished up going miles beyond him. I've often felt, "I want to keep going, keep pushing on, like that." All the radicals of the Reformation appealed to me, and not just – I hope – because I'm "bolshie-minded." I found that the radicals rediscovered truth which was buried under the ecclesiasticism of the medieval Church.

I was "over the moon" to discover that there were people who were putting the primacy of the New Testament over the Old in interpretation – because that is fundamental to my whole Christ-centred interpretation of the Bible. There are things in the Old Testament which are as yet sub-Christian and need to be revamped by the addition of Christ, especially with regards to the law. At Ichthus, we try to interpret the Old Testament in concordance with the New, rather than in contradiction to it. I was thrilled to find that the Anabaptists were bold enough to say such a thing, because I would get so misunderstood in conservative evangelical quarters for saying it. If, as Jesus says "all scriptures testify" of him, then scriptures without Christ are less than whole truth. He came to complete (fulfil) them.

Twenty years ago, I could sit in a room full of clergy, and as they went round describing who they were and their backgrounds, I described my theology as "Anabaptist," and I was mocked. It wouldn't happen today, but then many clergy were ignorant of the Anabaptist story. I knew all their disastrous church history plus that of the radicals; they didn't bother to find out about mine – other than Münster. But I know where I belong, whereas if you don't know where you belong you are vulnerable. I believe it is important for "new churches" and "new" historic churches to understand the authenticity, historicity and respectability of the theology and practice they inherit.

The Anabaptists had an evangelistic zeal that Europe still needs. At Zollikon in Switzerland the early Anabaptists started running through the village, even though it was night, telling people about Jesus because of their experience of joy and the presence of God. That kind of thing has always happened when the Spirit of God moves, and it's something that must be recovered if we are going to evangelise the world. Anabaptism brought a kind of egalitarianism, a breaking of the medieval threefold structure of noble, priest and peasant. It was a people's movement, not a clergy careerism.

There is much about the Anabaptism movement which is fundamentally a biblical-style church. Any form of recovery or restorationism (in which even many territorial churches also now believe) has got a historical model in Anabaptism which other churches can draw from and be blessed by. Anabaptism is for today. What the Anabaptists died for is now being taken on board right across the Church from Catholics through to the far left. People are imbibing it and beginning to try to live it – and sometimes pretending it was theirs all the time! That is part of the restoration God is giving us, bringing us back to something like Anabaptist-style church in all the churches.

A Sort of Homecoming
Andrew Francis, Sevenoaks

Andrew Francis is part of the leadership team at Christ Church, Sevenoaks, is involved in two training networks and is part-time Development Worker for the Anabaptist Network.

Have you ever come back to a place or a people that feels like home? I have, and it is called "Anabaptism."

I grew up in a small British believers-baptist denomination called the Churches of Christ. I later learned that they were part of the "Restorationist" movement, seeking to restore New Testament Christianity and patterns of biblical community. What I vividly remember are congregations which felt like family, in which rich and poor shared, as well as national and/or regional gatherings with vibrant participatory worship and missionary challenges.

As I approached teenage years, my father began tutoring in the Selly Oak Colleges. There I gained a picture of the world Church as students came from more countries than I knew existed. Visitors of

all races to our table were welcomed just as in my former grandparents'
home a few miles away in downtown Birmingham. Neo-Marxism and
monetarism vied with my spirituality to declare their priority. Events
like Greenbelt, Spring Harvest and friends joining "house churches"
gave me a renewed vision of "church as community." Five years of
working within industrial relations while living and worshipping in the
inner city confirmed Jesus' call to ministry.

The past is flooded with people, faces and places – all challenging
the way of being disciples together. Anabaptists were dismissed by
church history lecturers, but not forgotten. Long evenings of talk at
Taizé and Iona forged a thirst for something more. I met a former
hippy who introduced me to the work of Ben Zablocki, a sociologist,
who wrote a book about the Bruderhof – *The Joyful Community.* Who
were these people? What are they about?

Deep down, something was missing in the denominationalism of
my everyday existence as an ordained minister. Too many folk had
wanted me to be chaplain to their religious club. Three years of work
encouraging small inner-city Leeds congregations into obedient
renewal showed me better alternatives. Then a local Baptist leader
reminded me that I had yet to involve our folk in *Workshop.* This
Christian discipleship and leadership training course changed the
direction for good. Its director welcomed me and enthused some of
our congregation into new directions for the Lord. My wife Pat would
return from each *Workshop* weekend with another bag of books that
we would pore over. So many were by Anabaptists and then someone
gave me a form to subscribe to *Anabaptism Today.* These people
believed what I believed and wanted the kind of Kingdom
communities and congregations which I needed to be part of.

Undertaking the MTh course in Baptist and Anabaptist Studies at
Spurgeon's College has helped me realise the breadth of the
Anabaptist vision and its application to British Christianity now.
What has been very humbling is that others have invited me to share
directly in the development of the UK Anabaptist Network. As one
journeys, meeting so many like-minded people all seeking new
frameworks for our discipleship has not simply been refreshingly
challenging; it has been a sort of homecoming.

The Story So Far
John Freeman, Eastwood, Essex

John Freeman is a consultant in local government and a member of an Elim Pentecostal church.

The title of the book, *Coming Home*, seems very appropriate as a description of our experience of discovering Anabaptism. My wife Sally and I are, however, still only "coming." We haven't found home yet, but we know it's there somewhere. It must be.

We have both been Christians for nearly twenty years. We have experienced a number of different traditions, from Baptist to house church, different forms of worship, different teachings, styles, emphases. These differences seemed to matter so much – belief in and practice of the gifts of the Spirit, an emphasis on "freedom in worship," a zeal for numeric growth, getting into the "Toronto Blessing." Yet through all these experiences we both knew there had to be more.

Sally in particular had always been a "friendship evangelist" and we had both found ourselves gladly developing an "open door" lifestyle with a growing tendency to befriend the poor, the weak and the marginalised. However, the more this lifestyle developed the more we found ourselves being marginalised from the rest of the church! We found ourselves bringing many different people to all manner of so-called "low key" evangelistic events, only to find such meetings increasingly embarrassing and to find that our friends were in fact not being drawn into the church that we were "members" of, but were being drawn into "community" with us. They were finding a new identity – they were learning to belong.

We were already struggling to make sense of all this when we discovered Anabaptism. At first, I was somewhat uninterested. I was always looking for the "new" thing God was doing, longing for the prophetic, longing to tune into God's new strategy. Then as Sally and I talked together for hours on end and poured out our hearts to each other, read books and took time to reflect, we realised the truth had been there all along. It staggered me to realise that the Church had had this revelation for over three hundred ears and had somehow managed to ignore it. It is hard to put this revelation into a form of words that adequately express it, but the following points are an attempt:

• The teachings, sayings and stories that Jesus told came alive for us. We did not need to shy away from them, but could grasp them in all their acutely challenging glory – and live them out – yes, this was possible!

• The priesthood of all believers is not about personal freedom to achieve an individual spiritual experience but about a corporate experience of belonging to Jesus together that naturally overflows into worshipping together, praying for each other and serving each other.

• Church is not about meetings. It is about our relationship together with God and our relationships with each other and all those round us. Building church is about building community. Our meetings can then be an expression of our love for Jesus and each other and will naturally be interactive, participatory and maybe even events to be looked forward to!

• The way forward was not to copy the bits of *Acts 2–4* that seem relevant to our culture, but is actually far more radical. Just as the Holy Spirit led those early disciples quite naturally into sharing common goods and their whole lives together in inclusive community to build a new culture, so is he now. This is not about changing society, but is about building a new radical community within our society. This will be revival!

We will continue to search for home – like the kingdom of God, it's at hand!

What Makes Anabaptists so Annoying?
Ruth Gouldbourne, Bristol

Ruth Gouldbourne is Tutor in Church History in the Bristol Baptist College and a Baptist minister.

I think I was ten or eleven, and the family was on our annual holiday. This year we were travelling in northern Germany, dividing our time between finding swimming pools and looking at sites of historical interest. On this day, which was unbearably hot, I was standing with my father in the middle of the town square waiting for my mother and sister to return from some shopping. "Look up at that spire," said my father. "Do you see those cages? That was where the captured Anabaptists were hung on display." We were spending a few days in Münster, and it was the first time I had heard of the Anabaptists as a group of real people rather than a name for my sister (Ann). My father told me as much of the story as a ten-year-old could pay attention to, and I started to wonder just what kind of people these could be that everybody hated and feared so much.

Fifteen years later, I started a course in Reformation history as part of my theological degree, and the Anabaptists recurred to my consciousness. I found in them a welcome antidote to the very high Anglicanism of the college, always a little uncomfortable to a Baptist. And again, I found myself puzzled about why a group, which seemed so innocuous, was so hated and feared. This time the puzzlement became so insistent that it became part of the desire to do further academic research, and led to my current PhD work.

However, I found that an interest in the Anabaptists could not be limited to an antiquarian one, especially as I was serving in a local pastorate and beginning to find that reflection on the meaning and practice of the nature of the Church was an immediate issue. It was about this time that the Anabaptist Network was formed and I was able to join a group. Here I found a space where my historical interest and my pastoral and personal concern in the nature of discipleship and Church came together.

Since then I have found my interest in and drawing from the Anabaptist tradition has become both more focused and more frustrating. As I have become more shaped by the tradition, and found that the ideas have become more and more important to me, partly through the discussions with others in the Network, so I have found my discontent with my present experience of church life and my own level of commitment has grown. In that way, I would not say that my involvement with Anabaptist ideas and people has been an unmixed comfort; in fact, my original impression has stayed with me. What is it about these people that makes them so annoying? But I have made some progress – what makes them so annoying is that they challenge, undermine and de-centre so much of what I and others take for granted about the way of being Christian at this time and in my place. To be involved with Anabaptist ideas does not make for a comfortable life – thank God.

Dirk Willems Arrested Me
Gilly Greenwood, London

Gilly Greenwood attended the Wood Green Mennonite Church, promoted Workshop, is now a homemaker and part of an Anglican parish church (without being Anglican!).

I came across the Anabaptists in the context of a history lesson. If it wasn't for Dirk Willems' courageous and merciful action, I don't think I would have been arrested by Anabaptists at all; they would have merged into the tough times of post-Reformation Europe.

But Dirk's choice intrigued me, and through the study course *Workshop* I started to think about peace-making. I met blue-blooded Mennonites, I ventured to the London Mennonite Centre for training/ learning days on the Sermon on the Mount, "Politics of Jesus," "Simple Lifestyle," and mediation work. I was strongly attracted to these people because they were gentle, and the ideas they explored taught me about the radical ways of non-violence in Jesus' life, and in Anabaptists' lives today.

Up until I met Anabaptists, I hadn't engaged with this Jesus and his followers who were learning to be gentle but firm and creative in the face of conflict and injustice. The impact has rooted my values in hope and prayer.

Longing for Authentic Christian Belonging and Discipleship
Brian Haymes, Bristol

Brian Haymes is Principal of the Bristol Baptist College and a Baptist minister.

There are several streams which flow into the river of my interest in Anabaptist thinking and practice.

I grew up in a Christian home and I am glad it was so. From the first, I was told the stories of Jesus. I experienced Christians as those who were to be trusted – no small matter for a child growing up in the war years.

My coming to personal faith and believers' baptism was in a local church of considerable size and affluence. Within the fellowship I received care and good teaching, with living illustrations of the practice of discipleship. For example, our youth groups were involved in the redecorating of publicly owned homes where such work could not be afforded. It was the beginning of a conscious awareness that to follow Christ meant a different way of life, related to values which stand in challenge to prevailing assumptions. I recall the puzzles of teenage years when I contrasted the teaching of Jesus in the Gospels with the lifestyle and expectations of the members, many of whom I none the less admired. I eventually left the school army cadet force for what I now see were primitive but none the less genuinely theological reasons.

I believed myself called to be a Baptist minister. In my studies in college in preparation for ministry I found the Anabaptists of history more interesting than the magisterial reformers. It was their emphasis on the practice of discipleship which struck me as significant. I became more consciously aware of what I had received in being nurtured by devout Christians who implicitly gave me a sense of the necessity and vitality of community. Living in the community of the college I found an exciting challenge and, at times, a powerful learning context. It was another way in which I found myself facing the questions not only about belief but also discipleship and the contexts in which faith in God flourished.

Eventually I became a local Baptist pastor. My pastoral experience meant I was constantly asking about the nature of the true Church, its membership and its ministry. Questions about Church as community, as encouraging and supporting discipleship, being the context where people worked out the consequences of naming Jesus as Lord in baptism, were the real issues of the everyday. All this was at its sharpest when I was ministering in a large central context with the challenge to "turn this congregation into a church." The inherited forms of Church I discovered could frustrate community growth and so prevent or hinder the more radical questions of Christian commitment ever being asked.

In one congregation I served there were some members who were thinking about forming an intentional community. They knew my restlessness about the accepted forms of church life. I also knew how other members found the more radical and communitarian ideas we discussed disturbing. All the time I was aware that, in whatever form, the Church was losing touch with the wider community of the world in a bad sense. The big professional forms of evangelism did not seem effectively to meet this challenge. One of my pastorates was in a multicultural environment. It meant that the question of Christian distinctiveness was sharp. Answering it involved going back to fundamental issues concerning the Christian life itself.

Theologically I became increasingly interested in the relation of faith and action, belief and ethics. I had the opportunity to engage in some postgraduate theological study and took the opportunity to work on the question of what knowing God means. I was struck by the fact that in the Bible intellectual, experiential ways of knowing God were all of a part with a strong emphasis on practice. Knowing God was something you did! There was no knowing of God without faithful discipleship, nor a community which made this possible by retelling the story in worship and supporting one another in fellowship.

I was invited to teach in a theological college, concentrating on ethics. This brought me to look again at the Anabaptist traditions as re-expressed by John Howard Yoder and Stanley Hauerwas and others. From this work there grew the conviction that here is a massively significant approach to being Christian disciples in the post-Constantinian, post-Christian age. I longed to be part of a church that shaped its life and goals in this way.

I had a year as President of the Baptist Union of Great Britain, visiting many churches and talking with a wide cross-section of members. I was struck by their loyalty but also their restless desire for the experience of church to be different. Their longing was not simply for more heightened experiences, nor for more aggressive religious enterprises, but for a more authentic sense of Christian belonging and discipleship.

Through all these years I have been blessed by knowing and receiving the friendship of some fine Christians who exemplify this tradition of faith. They have made the love of God in Christ real to me. They have made the experience of being church liberating. Their realism and faithfulness together I find inspiring and an abiding source of gratitude to God.

A Faith Expressed in Real Life
Chris Horton, Wolverhampton

Chris Horton works as a lawyer in industry and, with his wife and three children, worships with an Anglican congregation in inner-city Wolverhampton.

I first became aware of the Anabaptists while studying for A-level history at school. I was already a Christian of fairly radical House Church persuasion, though at the age of seventeen I was in the happy position of being in contact with various Anglican, Baptist, Brethren and Pentecostal groups, and I even enjoyed reading a little Orthodox theology for good measure. The Anabaptists struck a chord with me, as the radical outsiders who seemed to be ahead of their time. I found myself thinking "that's what I believe" of some of their emphases.

But there was too little time to get beyond a brief glimpse. Besides, even A-level history is quite limited and history in the textbooks is the story of the rich and powerful. Later in my history studies, I found the religious radicals in England in the seventeenth century to be easier to study in detail and at that time a more direct inspiration and example.

Years later, when I was married with three young children and discovering by trial and error how to help lead a church congregation, I rediscovered the Anabaptists. In the limited time I had, often during lunch breaks at work, I was trying to wrestle with some theological issues of great practical importance: How should we as Christians seek to influence society and political powers? What success should we look for? Is the Church merely trying to save some souls before the world is destroyed or are we now part of a new creation which will be completed when Jesus returns? How do evangelism and social action interrelate? My wife and I had concluded that the Good News is especially for the poor and we wanted to lead the congregation into some forms of service of the poor as well as evangelism. But it was important to us to have a biblical understanding on these and similar questions.

A friend directed me to some helpful books and enabled me to think through the issues in a biblical way. I was fascinated to discover that the most helpful ideas came from writers who were self-consciously heirs of the Anabaptists. And I was delighted to discover that I had over the years developed (more by "accident" than design) an approach to the Scriptures which seemed the same as the Anabaptists.

This time I gave the Anabaptists a bit more time to speak into my own concerns and interests than I had at school. The Anabaptist Network was just starting and I joined the Sheffield study group, near to where I worked at the time. At the first meeting I heard the story of Dirk Willems clearly and powerfully told. It sums up so much of the Anabaptist approach. In fact it provides a preacher with a story to illustrate several different themes! But for me it is an example of the help Anabaptism can be:

• it demonstrates that commitment to Jesus and the gospel is a matter of action, as well as intellectual belief: good works are the proper consequence of faith;

• it is an inspiring example;

• it shows the importance of settling in our hearts the important issues of obedience and faith before the crisis comes, while there is opportunity; and

• its power is carried in story form, not in theoretical preaching: real-life godliness is what communicates to real people, not just words.

In the following months I enjoyed the friendship and stimulation of the group, usually based upon some aspect of Anabaptist history, but seeking to discover what it means to follow Jesus today. My questions were answered only partly by a growing theological understanding and only partly as a result of intellectual debate. More important was hearing the stories of ordinary saints in the past and working out in practice how God wants to develop our own stories in the present and future. The four aspects of the impact Dirk Willems' story had on me continue to be the benefit of meeting with others of like mind to discover more of radical discipleship.

The practical results were greater confidence in encouraging our local congregation to be radical, to put faith into practice and, in particular, to expect to care for the poor and lonely, whether or not the caring was connected with any evangelistic opportunity. We became confident that the results do not determine the acts of obedience and love: they should spring from lives committed to God. So the church became known as a group which could be relied upon to help with emergency grocery supplies when the benefit system could not move fast enough, and as an open and friendly group even if the gospel message was not received.

We have since moved as a family to the West Midlands and have enjoyed the meetings with the Midlands study group, which has more emphasis on being a small community/extended family, as well as discussing what it means to build community in a fragmented world. Times of laughter around a meal table and prayer are an important part of the mixture. While a group like this cannot replace church involvement, it does have many of its features. But the main significance is that the discussions are rooted in real life. As many of the sixteenth-century Anabaptists found, only faith based on revelation and knowing God but expressed in real life will stand the test.

The Church will Always Need Provocative and Challenging Groups
Angela Hughes, Leeds

Angela Hughes is a non-stipendiary minister within the United Reformed Church and is attached to the Wigton Moor URC, Leeds.

My story is a personal one, but I can certainly confirm that *Workshop* should carry a "health warning!" So where to begin? Educated in a convent, nurtured within a local Baptist congregation (Stanmore, Middlesex) and with non-church going parents, there had always been unresolved questions as I sought to make sense of, and live out, my Christian faith.

At eighteen I was baptised as a believer and then marriage and a new job for Donald, my husband, took us to Leeds in 1960. Here we became deeply involved in the planting of a new church on a new estate. We both felt that it was more important to be part of a local church than to remain in any particular tradition and so we became Congregationalists – soon to become part of the United Reformed Church.

Unexpectedly, we remained in Leeds and over the years we both took an active part in the development and growth of this new church. Through good times and bad, there was always a strong sustaining faith underpinning all that I did – but, for me, the questions did not go away. Then in 1989 I was asked to be Church Secretary and an Elder of the church. I reluctantly agreed, and this step marked the beginning of a period of growth and change.

The church discovered *Workshop* and four of us took the plunge and enrolled for it. My dilemma of different traditions of belief and practice suddenly became a rich and diverse resource. A long-standing conflict between personal salvation and social justice was reconciled. Where was the problem? Action must surely follow belief – look at the Anabaptists! The teaching was broad-based and served to enlarge the vision of traditionalist and of charismatic – and I really liked that. I longed, and still long, for more people to grasp the bigger picture of the kingdom beyond our denominational differences.

Anabaptist and Mennonite teaching made so much sense. It enabled me to discover a faith that was not something I constantly strove to achieve but that was part of me. It gave my life a wholeness and this was incredibly liberating. I went to the local Leeds Anabaptist study group. This became for me a source of refreshment and increasing interest. My interest (I am ashamed to say) was not in the history of the Anabaptists but in the insights that they can offer us today as we work out ways to be the Church in today's world. I believe the Church will always need provocative and challenging groups – like the Anabaptists. I believe too that we need the tradition and orthodoxy of the Established Church – that each has its role and place as we work for the kingdom.

The advice to us on the *Workshop* course was to work in the place where God had set us. I am now an ordained non-stipendiary minister within the United Reformed Church. I have a ministry within the Leeds District Council of the URC, working with individual churches on a specific task for a set period of time. My role is to encourage, facilitate, resource, enable, sometimes to disturb, always to challenge – it is to discover vision but also to enable the congregation to make their vision become real. My conviction that we are all "called" remains firm and the attractiveness of a distinctive community of disciples in which we can be sustained and nurtured to serve in the world remains an appealing one. The challenge for me now is to explore the ways in which such communities can engage with today's society.

Drawn to Anabaptism by the Heroism
of Those who Risked All
Duncan Johnstone,
West Yorkshire

Duncan Johnstone is minister of the Sutton-in-Craven and Glusburn Baptist Churches, West Yorkshire.

I have a photograph which greatly amuses my children. It shows me gazing spellbound at the house in Zürich once occupied by Conrad Grebel, while my wife looks in the window of the antique shop next door!

That was in 1994. My interest began with the *bête noire* of Anabaptism. In 1965, I discovered a novel by Peter Vansittart entitled *The Friends of God*. The story concerned a disillusioned nobleman who, following the Peasants' Wars, searches for a new meaning to life. His wanderings bring him to Münster. For the first time I encountered the name that for years afterwards would be used to justify all manner of barbarities against those disparate groups labelled Anabaptist. As the pages of the novel sped past I learned of fanaticism and bravery, of superstition and hocus-pocus, and finally of betrayal, degradation and death.

I wanted to know more about these strange, exciting people. I read *The Rise and Fall of the Anabaptists*, by E. Belfort Bax, published in 1903, more than three quarters of which is just about Münster. I read this book in 1966 – and re-read it in 1994. Unbalanced as it is for the full Anabaptist story, it paints a surprisingly sympathetic picture of John of Leyden and his fellow "apostles," arguing, surely with some justice, that the crimes of the Münster Anabaptists were certainly no greater than those of their persecutors, and conceivably more pardonable. In neither of these books did I learn much about Grebel, Sattler or Denck – but I was encouraged to read further.

My search has gone on, and in 1994 I spent a sabbatical at the International Baptist Seminary then based in Ruschlikon, near Zürich. And to Zürich I often went – to the Grossmunster in which

Zwingli preached, to the street behind, where Felix Mantz lived and the first modern believers' baptisms took place, to the river in front, where the same Felix Mantz was drowned – the first protestant to be killed by Protestants. I visited these places and others: Conrad Grebel's home, where a local asked me who he was (!) – and where my wife could look at antiques (!); Zollikon, where early baptisms and the first Lord's Supper were performed; and a cave way out in the country, where the persecuted believers met to worship.

My sabbatical work was to read about the first generation of Anabaptists – and compile a chronology of the events of the Radical Reformation during "the Zwingli Years" – 1519 to 1531, Zwingli's time in Zürich, when those men who had at first been his disciples moved away from his cautious policy to seek a full scale reform of Christendom.

So it has been mostly Anabaptist history which has fascinated me. And also the fact that these so-called "step-children of the Reformation" were just that, ill at ease with the world and the church; part of the church, yet alien to it. Since then I have met people who share my interest in some aspect of this great movement – and we seem to share something else too. The sense of not quite "fitting in" with the church as we find it, not being in total accord with any section of it, passing strangers in what passes for Christendom.

We were all initially drawn to Anabaptism for different reasons – some for its challenging and diverse theology, some for its stance on peace (though not all Anabaptists – Münster apart – were pacifists), some for its challenge to today's church. For me, it was the heroism of those first Anabaptists who risked all in order to be loyal to Jesus Christ as they understood him.

The Believers' Church Needs to Act Radically
Keith G. Jones, Didcot

Keith Jones is Rector of the International Baptist Theological Seminary, Prague, and a Baptist minis-

During my time as a theological student at the Northern Baptist College in the early 1970s I decided to take as my "special" subject church history. I already had a deep interest in Baptist history and principles and had discovered something of the story of the English Baptists, and, in particular, the General Baptists of the New Connexion, from which my home church had sprung.

I had understood that the General Baptists had come to their views about the baptism of believers while in exile in Holland and that they had been influenced by the Mennonite community, with whom they had taken refuge. However, despite doing Reformation history in the University, with specialist Reformation scholars, only passing reference was made to the radicals of the Reformation, the Anabaptists. The whole concentration of concern was on the Magisterial Reformers, particularly Luther and Calvin.

At the same time, my college principal encouraged me to do further academic study. In reflection on ethics, I had been drawn to themes of peace and to a querying of the just war theory, which had been one segment of my undergraduate course. I was, therefore, attracted to the School of Peace Studies in the University of Bradford and the masters course offered there by advanced study.

I was accepted for the course and met the professor, the outstanding Quaker, Adam Curle. His book *Mystics and Militants* had an important influence on me. My work in the school made me reflect in depth on the life of Martin Luther King and on the radical stand taken by some of the lesser known early Baptist missionaries in Sierra Leone. The whole Bradford experience was a key one to me as the academic work, the involvement in the postgraduate community and the stimulus and challenge of non-believers, including my personal tutor, a South African Marxist, caused me to ask radical questions about my

Christian belief and set me to looking more closely at the radical Anabaptist heritage which was mine, but about which I knew little.

Searching for a book to read for Lent in 1982 in my local SPCK Bookshop, I came across *The Politics of Jesus*, by John Howard Yoder. I found this a very stimulating book and the exegesis of Yoder stimulated my preaching as I visited the churches of Yorkshire Sunday by Sunday.

That question I asked in the School of Peace Studies now began to be answered for me and two years later in the autumn of 1984, when I had my first sabbatical, I went to Rüschlikon, the International Baptist Seminary on the side of the Zürichsee in Switzerland. It was the year to celebrate the five hundredth anniversary of the birth of Zwingli, and the Professor of Church History was the renowned Wayne Pipkin. In my three months in Switzerland many things began to fall into place. With Wayne Pipkin in a postgraduate seminar a handful of us explored the significance of Zwingli and the Anabaptists who parted ways with him. A Swedish student, Magnus Lindvall, was working on a dissertation on Pilgram Marpeck, and now the Radical Reformation, my peace concerns, my appreciation of the truly different nature of the believers' church model all began to slip into a coherent framework. The writings of Christopher Hill about the radicals of the English Reformation helped me understand better the concerns and the subculture of the radical and Anabaptist groupings during the period of the Reformation in England.

In Leeds, where I then lived, a network of people interested in the story of the Anabaptists and the contemporary application of their insights provided further stimulus, and my preaching and contribution to discussions about Baptist mission strategy began to reflect more obviously my interest in the radical reformers.

The 1990s has brought opportunity to become involved in the Anabaptist Network and to share in the convening of the Anabaptist Theological Study Circle, to read more widely, to talk more extensively and to experiment more courageously with insights from the Anabaptists.

My conviction is now that Ernest Payne was right when he took the view that "ideas have wings" and that the early English Baptists were influenced by the continental Anabaptists. This is not the received wisdom in some quarters. Today, I contend passionately that the believers' church needs to act radically to become the sort of missionary congregations which can have an impact in our post-modern, post-Christendom world. Anabaptist insights, it seems to me, have much to teach us and I am on a pilgrimage where my own ministry is being increasingly challenged and shaped by their witness.

A Vision of the Wholeness of Life and Faith
Pippa Julings, Leeds

Pippa Julings is an art student and mother who worships in an Anglican church.

My story of active involvement with Anabaptists (Mennonites) stretches through the decade of the 1980s. During this time I was involved, with others, in a justice and peace networking group of Christians called *Aslan Education Unit.* For myself, much of the personal energy and inspiration for this came from what I learnt from the London Mennonite Centre.

In 1980, I was recently married, with a small business selling third world crafts, as well as an active interest in local inner-city Liberal politics. In 1978, a group had formed around Ron Sider's book, *Rich Christians in an Age of Hunger,* which raised many questions for me about faith and injustice in the modern world. At that time we encountered quite some opposition to our activist Christianity, which for many did not appear to be sufficiently biblically or spiritually rooted, or "too political." There was a clear but inactivated need to get justice issues out of fringe meetings and into the worship of the whole Church.

From this background we were introduced, via the Greenbelt Festival, to the resources and history of the London Mennonite Centre. This was a vital encounter, and opened up for us many areas – hospitality, openness to questioning, the internationalism, worship and ecumenical awareness of this small community. Here was a biblical and spiritual rootedness for which I craved, with an unappreciated history and a mass of literature to explore and share with others.

There began an active partnership between Leeds and the Centre, with various speakers doing a series of teaching events to support and give biblical framework to the work of *Aslan*. When one of these spoke at the launch of a new inter-church peace group for Leeds, it wasn't known that a few months later we would be thrown into the Falklands War. At a key gathering in 1984, the catch word was "It all fits together!" and we caught a glimpse of Christians across the denominations engaging with important issues of the day in worship, dance and drama. One local charismatic Anglican church refused our offer of worship on peace issues, unemployment or world development, but were able to accept one on "worship and justice." Such was the mood of the times, which Mennonite witness caught. It would have been good then to have had today's resources of an Anabaptist network and magazine, to feed into the upsurge of interest in Leeds in the mid-1980s.

Over the years, I continued to learn from friends at the Centre, taking part in debates on their outreach programme, and assisting with production of teaching materials. It was there we picked up interest in the Myers Briggs personality typing, the practice of discussion over a good shared meal ("Table Talks"), various traditions of contemplative prayer and many other avenues of personal growth. Mennonite experience also fed my contribution to our local parish church, an inner-city Anglican church open to new experiences of worship and faith. Here we pioneered work with children, lay leaders and reconciliation between different "factions" over Remembrance Day. I found Mennonite understandings of the Bible and storytelling expressed by phrases such as "concrete grace" or "social holiness" to be received with joy and openness here, in a way that formal statements of doctrine were not.

I went on to have four children, and my active involvement with Mennonites ceased, other than hosting the local Anabaptist Study Group for a while. What are the challenges they leave me with? There is a vision for family and congregational life which I feel energised by, but have not managed to incarnate! Anabaptist stories and insights on issues of power, consensus decision-making, peacemaking and active listening seem in my experience to be needed today more than ever, and I applaud the London Mennonite Centre's focus on these questions. Although I am no longer actively involved, it is to be hoped that the vision of the wholeness of life and faith which I gained from an intense period of Anabaptist experience stays with me, and colours my ongoing struggles of church, work and family life.

Discovering Jesusness
Juliet Kilpin, East London

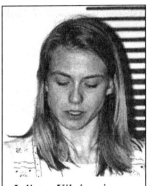

Juliet Kilpin is co-ordinator of Urban Expression, an inner-city church planting initiative in Shadwell, East London.

I think it must have been at Spurgeon's College that I first encountered Anabaptism, but I don't think it was until right at the end of my studies, or even when I had left, that I realised that much of what my tutor had been teaching or exposing us to was Anabaptist. Often he would give us different case studies where we would look at a real-life issue or problem. There would be different ways of sorting it out which we would have to reflect and comment on. But after this he would often suggest an extra option, which would always seem like the natural option to me, but wasn't necessarily one of the regular options that Christians considered. Looking back, I realised that all these extra options had tended to be Anabaptist!

What I've read up until now in Anabaptist teaching really just summarises everything that I'd thought previously but had never been able to categorise. I think that what really attracted me to the Anabaptists was the way that they brought everything back to the basics of what Jesus taught and what Christianity is fundamentally all about. They were very Christ-centred and took what he taught literally. They saw the Christian faith as being more than just on the surface – that it affects your whole life and needs to be expressed through every area of your life. For me, this means trying to express Jesus in everything I do. We call this "Jesusness" in our team.

Some things which were distinctive about the Anabaptists are affecting the way we are going about planting a church here in East London. One example is how our team is trying to explore the value of "community." The practice of community was something that I always felt was very important to church life but I never really saw it practised anywhere. Our goal is that, even though we don't have a building and have a low profile in the neighbourhood (compared with an established church), people will know who we are and will see our commitment to one another and will want to be part of this community. We see community as an inclusive thing, that people can be part of it and enjoy the benefits of it even if they are right at the very edge. As they hopefully come to understand more about Christ, they will move further in and choose to take on the responsibilities of belonging to community as well.

We also want to see the church that emerges being sacrificial, especially in terms of demonstrating our commitment towards one another, through sharing possessions and money, etc. So far, I think this has simply meant learning to be very honest about our financial situations, learning to ask for help when it is needed, and learning that "my" money isn't mine just to spend without consulting others, especially on big items. This means being accountable and being able to tell each other when we're not doing well. Rather than just leaving faith down to me and God, it's me and others and God, and they are free to interact with that relationship as well.

The thing that I get a bit nervous about with this Anabaptist stuff is that it seems to me that there's an awful lot of talking and not very much doing. And it really bugs me when people sit around talking about Anabaptist ideals and they don't express them. I can understand the tension if you're in a church that you're trying to move on or change. But personally I really struggle with this, because if we believe so fundamentally that this is the way church should be, then we need to be getting on and doing it. I don't want to leave it till I'm sixty to try something. That's something we have talked about as a team, that this is the best chance we will probably ever be given to create church the way we really believe it should be done and we don't want to blow it. And we would hate to look back in ten or twenty years' time and say we had this brilliant chance and we just created another boring church that isn't relevant or contextual.

I know that others commit themselves to reforming churches and I realise that both approaches are needed. But I guess that was the difference between Luther and the Anabaptists. I admire those people who can stay in a church in order to reform it when they don't compromise on what they believe. But I don't admire someone when they use their church situation as a cop-out from really stepping out and doing what they believe God is telling them to do. It's quite a safe position to be in, to be able to blame others for restricting you. But in church planting, as long as you've got supportive accountability, you've got no one else to blame but yourself!

A Renewed Sense of Calling
Vivienne Lassetter, Didcot

Viv Lassetter works for the Baptist Union as Ministries Adviser and is a Baptist minister.

I first heard of Anabaptism in the early 1980s. My minister would very often mention Anabaptism in his sermons. At that time I did not really grasp its significance, nor did I understand that I was taking part in a living history lesson. My birth roots are in Roman Catholicism, so coming to terms with contemporary nonconformism as I was beginning to know it was difficult enough.

Some years later, while I was a student at Northern Baptist College, two Mennonites came into my life. They modelled gentle assertiveness, poked fun, genuinely loved people, and lived the gospel ethos in a style hitherto unfamiliar to me. They came among us as Mennonite theologians with shared Anabaptist roots. We spent some time together discussing worshipping congregations. I shared my thoughts, ideas and longings, they shared their experiences. In the pastorate, I put my dreams into practice, having been encouraged and emboldened by our times together.

I wanted to explore the power of storytelling in worship, the place of symbolism, colour and play. I wondered about the effects of memory association and stories of faith as a congregation journeyed together trying to make sense of life and faith in a local context. One of my Mennonite friends spoke words of life and wisdom into my practice of ministry when she encouraged me to hold on to the sense of play she had perceived was present in the life of the church. It was just what I needed to hear!

In 1996, I went to the London Mennonite Centre to participate in a course on mediation and conflict skills training. This was to prove to be a very significant time for me. Along with a dozen or so others, I spent five intensive days learning the art of mediation; bringing people to consensus, using role play. During this week, ideas and ossibilities o ened u to me. I could see how much this ministr is needed in our churches. We learned how to be hard on issues, soft on people, skills I have used over and over again in all kinds of situations. Something happened to me during that week. I felt a very deep stirring within to learn all I could about this work, to get involved. I can only describe it as a renewed sense of calling.

Since that time I have had the opportunity to pass on what I learned to students at theological college and to a group of sixty ministers in the north-west of England. I have gained enough confidence to begin to write some material myself in order to contextualise areas of conflict in British Baptist churches. I am utterly committed to making mediation known to our denomination and to publicising the work of the London Mennonite Centre. My meeting with Mennonites and a renewed introduction to Anabaptism has opened up to me possibilities and insights to be worked out within my own tradition, not least in my preaching and in the way I relate to others.

To me Anabaptism stands for rootedness. It stands for attitudes and lifestyles tried and tested through the years. It stands for peaceful living, righteous thinking, political courage, strong relationships. Anabaptism is about caring community, thinking faith, costly Christian witness.

Anabaptism engages with the world today as it brings the lessons learned in the past to bear on church life in the 1990s. Anabaptism engages with our rootless culture through networks of storytellers and history-weavers. It empathises with, challenges and celebrates life and faith in educative and inclusive groups, open to all who care enough to want to join. These groups are challenging, stimulating, rewarding and threatening, and will probably change the life and ministries of those who belong. Anabaptism has shaped me, and I hope will go on doing so as long as I am prepared to grow.

Jesus' Call to Shalom: The Heart of the Gospel
Andrew Lewis-Smith, London

Andrew Lewis-Smith is a social worker who works part-time with Bridge Builders at the London Mennonite Centre.

I became a Christian on Thursday 20 October 1994. My conversion came towards the beginning of the phenomenon known as the "Toronto Blessing." Clearly, God was at work in me as I'm still not quite sure what prompted me to go on the Alpha course. Unlike many of the other participants, I had no sense of emptiness, of searching, of a need for healing. In fact I was pretty happy with life. However, there I was hearing and seeing things that only a few weeks earlier would have been an alien world. I can also say that I'd never heard or read about the Toronto Blessing. However on that Thursday, at precisely 3:00 p.m. while I was at home, with no external stimulation such as music, I began crying and knew with all of my being that I now believed. I did not know the theological terms, but I had become a disciple of Jesus.

Over the next few months I read voraciously and began to see the world very differently. I read theology books and the life stories of people such as Corrie Ten Boom, Sadhu Sundar Singh and Thomas Merton. However, I felt a certain uneasiness in both my reading and in my daily life as a Christian. Why did no one talk about peace issues? Why did people give me simplistic answers to complex questions such as how Christians relate and coexist with other religions? Looking back, I now realise that my faith was being threatened, as I was becoming frustrated and angry. The church that I saw in the world was not the church of Corrie Ten Boom and it did not seem to espouse the non-violence of Thomas Merton.

Fortunately, Maddy, whom I'm now married to, introduced me to a theology course called *Workshop*. I came across incredible teaching on peace and justice issues and a myriad of other topics. I bought books that I'd never seen in Christian bookshops – *The Upside-Down Kingdom* by Donald Kraybill, *The Politics of Jesus* by John Howard Yoder and *Rich Christians in an Age of Hunger* by Ron Sider. It is very difficult to covey the excitement I felt at discovering the Anabaptist legacy. Here, four hundred years on, was a movement which offered ideas, ways of being and amazing stories – and all in a European context.

I then met some Mennonites, my first experience of people who called themselves Anabaptists. Here were people who felt that the heart of the gospel was Jesus' call to peace and *shalom*. From that foundation flowed mission, lifestyle and the struggle to live a radical lifestyle.

I now work part-time with *Bridge Builders*, the Mennonite mediation and conflict resolution service. Not only do I have Jesus as my spiritual guide but also I have the privilege of meeting many wise, Spirit-filled and inspiring people. If you would have told me four years ago what I would be doing now, I would have laughed. However, I am now proud to say that I am a disciple of Jesus who walks in the Anabaptist tradition.

Tingling Excitement as to Where God is going to Lead us Next
Karl Longworth, Crewe

Karl Longworth is an instructor for ICI Bible Study (International Correspondence Institute) and is actively involved in a local Pentecostal church.

As a history teacher I had always been aware of the role of the Anabaptists and the Radical Reformation and, as a young Christian, I became interested in peace issues and in community. They led me to read some Anabaptist literature. While not adopting all Anabaptist viewpoints, the perspective given to me by these books has influenced the style and direction of my life.

During the 1980s we gave up our middle-class lifestyle to live and work in an Urban Priority Area. Many influences were at work here as I began to appreciate the concern God has for the poor and the oppressed. However, the work of people like Jim Wallis and *Grassroots Magazine*, and the values implanted in me by my awareness of Anabaptism all contributed to the birthing of this venture. The six years we spent in a downtown multi-ethnic part of Blackburn was a time of successes and failures, but it was also an attempt to be an arm of the Church in a radical way.

Since leaving Blackburn I have studied for a degree at Regent's Theological College in Nantwich and am working part-time as an instructor for ICI Bible Study. My deepening awareness of theology has again led me towards the Anabaptist viewpoints. I am avidly reading books by Brueggemann and various other theologians promoted by the Metanoia Book Service.

Again, as my understanding is being enriched by the radical theology of Anabaptist-influenced theology, I feel a tingling of excitement as to where God is going to lead us next. The early Anabaptists never seemed to have long to settle. They were uprooted by persecution, and had to flee to other places. So often in the Christian life we want to be static, but God calls us like the Israelites to leave the security of Egypt and move towards the Promised Land.

Radical Christianity is about growth and movement. Once we are static we "die." We have yet to hear where God will lead us. However, I am convinced that my Anabaptist-influenced understanding of the Bible will influence the direction taken.

My vision is for the churches to learn the lessons and implications embedded in the Anabaptist tradition. Issues like peacemaking, community, and the priesthood of all believers are vital to the well-being of the Church. Often as Christians we hang on to our own traditions and never look beyond. However, as a Pentecostal charismatic Christian, I believe the various movements and networks have much to learn from the Anabaptist tradition. Each one of us has to hear afresh what the Spirit is saying to the churches.

Anabaptist theology is not for the faint-hearted, but rather for those who are willing to be challenged.

Forming Communities of Faith that Incarnate the Gospel
Ewen MacDonald, Deptford, London

Ewen MacDonald is one of the leaders of the Deptford Park Church. He is pursuing God's call to ministry in the Moslem Turkic world.

I was brought up in a conservative evangelical background and associated church with a necessary boring prerequisite for a bite of the pie in the sky when you die. Despite this, my commitment to Christ at the age of thirteen was a very conscious and serious decision that did change my life permanently, and I embarked on a journey of discipleship that I am still on.

A key feature of the journey that has taken me to embrace Anabaptism is a need to reconcile what twentieth-century evangelicalism separated – the witness of the gospel to the poor in challenging injustice and the witness of the gospel in "saving souls." As I grew up, I associated the gospel of the poor with liberal Anglicanism. I associated the work of the

Holy Spirit with charismatic evangelicalism, and the two seemed to have no common ground.

My college years were turbulent for me, as I faced the stark reality that my evangelical faith was found wanting in compassion for the poor and for the developing world; it was also characterised by an uncritical conservatism towards the political world that in the 1980s was clearly in need of challenging. The issues of post-modernity which I feel we are all grappling with now, like it or not, led me to renounce my faith overnight, and for a year I looked for answers in all the places that students seem to look for them. It was only one night as I passionately argued against my Christian friends that the reality of my personal faith and love for Jesus gained mastery over the scepticism and cynicism that I had allowed to direct my path. As I once again embraced my faith, I tried to invite the Lord into my walk through the very confusing world that I had grown up in.

I found myself three years later planting a church in Deptford, south-east London with some college friends. The mother church allowed me to go on a year-long theology course to facilitate my church planting experience, and it was while doing this that I came across Anabaptism.

At college, I had been excited by learning of the Hussites in Bohemia in the fourteenth century and their stand against the corruption of the Roman Church, but I had been disappointed by their decline into armed warfare and nationalism. Similarly, the story of Luther I found exciting but had been terribly disappointed by his condemnation of the peasants in the revolt of 1525 and his subsequent resignation to be the puppet of the German political powers. Calvin's Geneva, with its burnings at the stake, seemed to complete the trend that beset these "great spiritual and theological" developments that we Evangelicals are supposed to be in such debt to. These giants that I could look back to in history seemed to require that I have an enormous spiritual blind spot; in order to appreciate their contribution to historical faith, I needed to ignore the wars, burnings (with green wood in the case of Calvin), torture, corruption and political intrigue associated with their names. Surely these people were not the last word on apostolic New Testament Christianity in the later Middle Ages?

One of the main leaders of the mother church spoke of finding a spiritual home in the historical tradition of the Anabaptists. He spoke of Menno Simons, Melchior Hoffman and others. I began to realise that there had been organised groups of believers who were aggressive in their passion for the gospel and seemed to have a lot in common with us. They considered themselves to be outside the corrupt church of the day. They believed that to be a follower of Christ one had to decide, instead of simply being born into a Christian state. They subsequently baptised adults. They had a passion for the Scriptures and they reached the common people. Their theological emphasis seemed to be resistant to Calvinistic fatalism and challenged the political powers instead of legitimising them. They believed in a radical communal lifestyle. I could well be at risk of idealising the early Anabaptists, but they appeared to me then to be a haven of truth, humility and peaceful sacrifice amidst a tragic and confusing European history. That same history sadly has all too often been synonymous with the Church, Catholic and Protestant. That was how Anabaptism first burst into my world view.

As a very busy Christian worker in inner London, my time to study theology was limited by the needs of the community I was serving. But I read *The Politics of Jesus*. This book had a profound effect on me. While embracing the gospel as good news to the poor, I felt we were aspiring to the kind of church growth and experience that simply emphasised numbers and supernatural experience. I was committed to a single-minded pragmatic attitude to seeing the gospel go out to all the world, but in this single-mindedness, what kind of gospel would it become? Amidst these kind of questions, the work of John Howard Yoder made a significant impression on me, and with it a renewed desire to look into Anabaptist theology as it addresses our present age.

The call to be a holy nation set apart for God seems to me to be a part of the gospel that the Anabaptists really understood. The culture they flourished in was very hostile to them. To be a Christian was in the understanding of the day to be a citizen of Christendom. Any attempt to establish spiritual life outside the precincts of the state Protestant or Catholic church was to claim citizenship of another nation. As a result, their heresy was to be dealt with as treason against the political establishment; their faith was inherently a political one, as it paid allegiance to another, rival kingdom. From this scenario it is clear that a commitment to pacifism followed. The kingdom they were part of was the peaceable kingdom of love that sacrificially followed the teachings of Jesus. This teaching could be radically followed, uncompromised by questions of how to make the teachings of Jesus apply to human political organisation founded on the need to coerce in order to bring order. It is this emphasis that has helped me enormously in understanding present questions and issues. The Anabaptists seemed to be clear on where our loyalty truly lies as human beings enmeshed in hundreds of allegiances.

Christ's challenge to the rampant individualism of our day and its self-serving consequences seems to be articulated most effectively by neo-Anabaptists. Instead of negative criticism of the world and Church, Christ's call for us to be a body, a family, a community, both challenges and brings hope. Instead of the old divisions I mentioned earlier where "Evangelicals save souls and liberals are social workers," we are all called into forming a new community that witnesses God's truth in word, lifestyle and deed. Discipleship means that we are followers of Jesus before we are left- or right-wing. We have our own practices and customs as Christians that are strange to the world, which is inevitable as we are a people set apart. While earnestly desiring that "none should perish," the journey of faith will probably never be the choice of the majority. The urge to spread the gospel is best committed to forming communities of faith that incarnate the gospel, instead of only verbally communicating it.

Commitment to an Overflowing Love which Rejects Violence
Alastair McKay, London

Alastair McKay is a member of the Wood Green Mennonite Church who will complete an MA in Conflict Analysis and Transformation at Eastern Mennonite University in July 1999, before returning to work with the Bridge Builders service of the London Mennonite Centre.

My first contact with Anabaptists was when I heard two Mennonites preach in York in 1984, soon after I had started following Jesus. I then took part in a Saturday seminar in York run by people from the London Mennonite Fellowship (as it then was).

At the end of December 1989, I organised a walking holiday in Yorkshire with a friend, who invited a certain Sue Lee along as one of the party. Sue and I hit it off. I found out that she worshipped with the Mennonites (although was not a member of the congregation), and Sue likes to tell that one of my early chat-up lines was "I'd really like to visit your church." However, I was genuinely interested in visiting the congregation due to my earlier contacts with it – even if there was also another dimension to the request!

Within three or four months, Sue had agreed to marry me. We had to decide where to live, North London where she was, or South London where I was. Sue was unable to feel at home in the large, charismatic Anglican congregation I was part of, which had lengthy services. In contrast, I liked the small Mennonite fellowship, being drawn by the quality of relationships. So it proved a relatively easy choice to join the Mennonites, and to live in North London. The major losses of the shift for me were of the whole charismatic dimension to my corporate experience of the church, something I am still sad about, and of a strongly liturgical element to worship, which I still miss.

Having initially been attracted by the quality and character of individual people and their relationships, I then attended a few group study sessions at the London Mennonite Centre, looking at the early

Anabaptists. What an exciting revelation! Here were Christians who seemed to resemble those I read about in Acts, but living 1,500 years later and being persecuted, not by Romans and Jews, but by others who called themselves Christian. What a powerful testimony to God's love and character these early Anabaptists gave! Through these study sessions my interest was whetted for Anabaptist history and theology.

The Anabaptist heritage has reinforced my sense of the centrality of Jesus, particularly his whole life and teaching as a model and guide for us. It has helped me to understand the importance of the Church and the corporate nature of (among other things) Christian discipleship, worship and hermeneutics. It has also challenged my thinking in a number of areas, particularly on issues of coercion and non-violence – whether manifest in my innermost being and thinking, or through actual physical expression – and I have come to see the way of Jesus as a commitment to an overflowing love which completely rejects violence towards and coercion of other people, and instead pursues peace even with those who are one's enemies. What I have found helpful about the Anabaptist tradition is its embodiment of a way of discipleship and a form of biblical interpretation which takes Jesus and the Hebrew and Christian Scriptures seriously and seeks to live them out fully today. Here is a tradition which offers a meaningful and convincing way to aspire to follow Jesus thoroughly.

Then in February 1994, I took part in a three-day training course in mediation skills, organised by the London Mennonite Centre. I devoured the materials, ideas and practice we were offered. I was so excited. Suddenly, I had discovered what I wanted to be involved with – mediation and conflict transformation work. I felt that at long last I had found my work calling.

After a year of deliberation, a small group of us from the course set up a voluntary community mediation project to address neighbour disputes in the London Borough of Haringey. Within another year this proved to be non-viable because of the extensive nature of the other commitments of the core group of four people involved. However, the London Mennonite Centre had received a number of calls asking for training in handling conflict within the Church, and even one request to act as an intermediary in a large Baptist church on the verge of splitting. These pointers, along with our mutual interest in the area, led to our decision to try to reconstitute *Bridge Builders* as a service geared to offering training in handling conflict within congregations and a consultancy service for churches. I put together a grant application to Mennonite Central Committee (Europe) and an application to move to four days a week in my civil service work. When both applications were successful, we were able formally to launch the transformed *Bridge Builders* service in January 1996, staffed one day a week by me, with a similar time commitment from Nelson Kraybill, then Director of the London Mennonite Centre.

In 1996, my family and I visited the recently founded Conflict Transformation Program of Eastern Mennonite University in Harrisonburg, Virginia to explore the possibility of studying for an MA in Conflict Analysis and Transformation. In July 1997, we duly moved to Virginia for me to begin my studies, due for completion in July 1999, when we hope that I will return to head up a full-time *Bridge Builders* service at the London Mennonite Centre. The whole of my working-life's direction, and my orientation regarding conflict and disagreement, has been radically changed as has my whole theological outlook and my Christian identity. And I hope – unless Jesus returns or takes me early to himself – there is still much of this exciting journey which lies ahead, uncharted, and yet prepared by God. It is an adventure such as I had never foreseen, but for which I am heartily grateful to have the opportunity to journey in.

Models of Constructive Dissent
Justin Meggitt, Cambridge

Justin Meggitt is a Fellow of Jesus College, Cambridge.

I discovered Anabaptism by chance. When I was doing my A levels, I was forced to study the Reformation. Among the various books we had to read was G. R. Elton's *Reformation Europe*, a work which is extremely disparaging about Anabaptists. Frankly, as the rest of the Reformation had no appeal whatsoever to me (one side appeared as compromised as the other), and I had already grown to distrust Elton's views on most things, I thought that the Anabaptists must have had something extremely important to say. By luck, I managed to find some Bruderhof reprints of some early Anabaptist confessions in my local Scripture Union bookshop, and so began my interest in Anabaptism: the clarity and purpose of the faith was astonishing and the commitment to the peaceful kingdom, in the face of so much persecution, profoundly challenging. I have to say that I was not a Christian at this point (though I wasn't anti-Christian either), but the faith and determination of these Anabaptist testimonies was extremely appealing.

Anabaptism as a contemporary reality became real to me as I worked my way through an undergraduate degree in religious studies. The work of Mennonite scholars such as John Howard Yoder, in particular, but also Willard Swartley and others, gave me the support I needed to combine my awakening, critical faith with a commitment to the radical gospel that I felt pulsed through the Bible. The Anabaptist literature I acquired to supplement my reading lists taught me that intellectual, Christian and ethical integrity could go hand in hand.

Finally, as a result of a few speculative letters and the kindness of the Canadian government, I managed to acquire funding to attend Conrad Grebel College, Waterloo, Ontario, to pursue a Master of Theological Studies. That was a rare privilege, one for which I am extremely grateful and which continues to influence me, both personally and intellectually. Although my time there still fills me with mixed feelings (and has left me with some disillusionment, both with myself and with aspects of Anabaptism as actually lived out by the diverse communities that make up Canadian Mennonites), I certainly felt that that institution, and the many people associated with it, demonstrated the creativity and commitment which, at its best, Anabaptism can achieve: a true city on a hill.

And now. What is Anabaptism to me? Although I am a Quaker, and so have to part company with most Anabaptists over some central tenets of Anabaptism, I still consider the Anabaptist churches one of the most important models of constructive dissent which will become ever more important for Christians as we enter the new millennium. I am constantly aware of the parallels between the dynamics of Anabaptist faith and that of the earliest Christians, and it would be foolish of me not to admit that my work in biblical scholarship is influenced by the model of faith to which Anabaptism witnesses. The just and loving community that I see at the heart of Anabaptism, and its witness to sacrificial discipleship, is very precious to me and something that I am thankful to have encountered. My prayer is that others will be as privileged.

Taking Christ's Commands at His Word
Chris Metcalfe, Highbridge, Somerset

Chris Metcalfe is a retired British Telecom worker and a member of a Baptist church.

The Lord drew me into the kingdom at a Crusader camp in the summer of 1954. From the beginning, I found the way of the cross hard going, for I was a typical confused teenager of the 1950s. My family was like so many of the period: Christian as far as morals were concerned, but in everything else you did your own thing. If there was any God, materialism was that god.

The church I attended, the one to which I owed my spiritual survival, was an old-fashioned Anglican evangelical church, where one toed the party line, not thinking much for yourself, but following the orders that came from above. Suggestions that the church should have had all things in common definitely would not have been welcomed, as there were some very wealthy and high-salaried business types in the congregation.

At the age of twenty-one, I joined the merchant navy where I met and saw all sorts and conditions of men, and where the Lord in his grace kept my faith intact. After five years' seafaring, I came ashore and settled in Burnham-on-Sea, where I married and joined one of the local churches. I was fortunate to meet mature Christians who looked after me and pointed the way forward.

It was during this period that I began to question and see how one could follow Jesus in the 1970s. A large proportion of the members of my church were incomers, who had retired to Burnham and did not want any change in the church. My suggestions and criticisms were not well received, and I found myself isolated from most other church members and experienced at first hand the pain of rejection. In my fumbling way, I was groping towards a mutual way of life, a closer walk with the Lord and an openness between fellow believers; only in this way, it seemed to me, could the church meet the momentous challenges of the future.

Meanwhile I was helping to bring up a young family and also had to cope with the strains of earning a living, so my pilgrimage was anything but speedy. There were long periods when nothing seemed to happen and then, from time to time, something would happen, and a little bit of progress would be made. At the same time the Lord was dealing with me, disciplining me, making me depend on him, while within I was disappointed at the spiritual impotence of the church, its sitting at ease in Zion, and its lack of discipleship and struggle in the bland assurance of some church members that they were on the way to heaven at no cost to themselves. Cheap grace indeed.

If the church was to survive, it needed to attract younger people and, as if to illustrate the point, my own children ceased to attend. The culture was stuck in Edwardian times; it was not relevant to them. The search began for a form of church life which would meet the challenges of the late twentieth century, where one could be helped in one's Christian discipleship, and which would provide structure so that Christ's Body could be in a position to obey the Lord's commands.

The light dawned when I read *Living in Christian Community* by Art Gish, and through it I was introduced to the writings of modern Anabaptists like Eberhard Arnold. I learned something of Anabaptist history, where common men and women dared to take Christ's commands at his word. Their challenge to the state and Roman Catholic Churches was to result in vicious persecutions where no holds were barred and quite ordinary people full of the Holy Spirit maintained their faith and discipleship to the end. Their story is one of the neglected wonders of the Christian Church and, even more important, the path they have pioneered and the church principles they held on to are, in my estimation, the way forward for all Christians as they face the challenge of the twenty-first century.

Asking Distinctive Questions about Power
Bill Miller, Leamington Spa

Bill Miller is a probation officer and a Baptist lay leader.

I first came across the Anabaptists in the late 1980s, but only as dots on a map of Reformation Europe. I was perusing the *Lion Handbook History of Christianity* and was sufficiently intrigued by these specks of nonconformity to read the accompanying article by Alan Kreider and John Howard Yoder. What I read was very attractive, but two features of the Anabaptists prevented me, as an evangelical Anglican, from identifying with them too closely. One was their practice of "re-baptising" adults who had already been baptised as infants. The other was that they were a Christian grouping separated from modern Britain by both time and location. The Anabaptists were certainly of historical interest, and I had previously been unaware of their existence, but they did not impinge greatly on my twentieth-century English Christianity. Nevertheless, I knew enough about the Anabaptists for them to have earned my respect.

It was many years later that I experienced Anabaptism as a vibrant reality, which profoundly reshaped my thinking. In 1994-1995, I attended *Workshop*. I recall, on several occasions, feeling an almost physical sensation of being transfixed by Truth. I came to realise, over a number of months, that many of the insights, which I was finding most powerful and liberating, were rooted in Anabaptist thinking. It was a rediscovery of the gospel on a new level.

I had never agreed with the idea of an established church. As an Anglican, I had been firmly in favour of disestablishment. However, in 1994, this became an issue of conscience for me when I encountered Anabaptist thinking on the subject. How could a church have any real hope of being true to the gospel while it was tied to the powers of the status quo? I could not remain contented in the Church of England. It was relatively easy to make the change because I had only just moved to a new area of the country, and I soon settled into a Baptist church in Warwickshire.

Some members of this small church were a little bemused by me. I had arrived among them as a refugee from the Church of England over an issue of conscience, but the issue was not baptism. Rather, it was the logical outcome of a radically altered understanding of the Church and of the freedom that we have in Jesus Christ.

In establishing my sense of Anabaptist identity, the people who have been most significant have been the members of the West Midlands Anabaptist study group. This group first met in the autumn of 1995 and since then, we have met about eight times a year to share a meal, to break bread, to build friendships and to study together some aspect of the Christian life from an Anabaptist perspective. The early Anabaptists placed great emphasis on community, and it has been very important that our insights and ideas have been shaped in dialogue with one another in the context of committed friendships. Those times together have been very precious and I am profoundly grateful for the group. We try to explore together issues that are often being neglected by the wider Church.

I came to Anabaptism in 1994 immediately after completing a diploma in social work, which at that time was the required qualification to become a probation officer. My social work training had made me more aware of the significance of power in human relationships. So much began to fit into place when I reflected on how power was used by the Church and within the Church. It seemed to me that the fragrance of Jesus was most evident among Christian groups who had voluntarily laid aside power and coercion, or else who had had no opportunity to use them in the first place. Power was the way of the world, but vulnerability was the way of Jesus and his followers. Anabaptism was rooted in this rejection of coercive power.

As I have already said, discovering Anabaptism was rediscovering the gospel. There was a familiarity about it. As I told many of my friends when I was first discovering about Anabaptism, I did not fully understand it, but it smelt right. It felt exciting and challenging, and yet it was as though I had known about it before. It was new, and yet it was not new. Anabaptism was making sense of a number of glimpsed insights of the past. It was as though a distant memory was being brought to the forefront of my mind, and I believe that this was because in the Anabaptist heritage I recognised Jesus.

The stories of the early Anabaptists were inspiring. The story of Dirk Willems brought me to tears, because the story of Dirk's self-sacrificial love for his enemy is the story of Jesus. I had long struggled with the words of Jesus that we should love our enemies, and yet almost all the Christians I knew believed that killing could be justified. How could I love my enemies and also kill them? One morning in the bath I had a moment of revelation when I realised with great joy that if I loved my enemies, then I could not kill them. The Anabaptists had led the way and given me an example to follow. In fact they were exemplifying the way of the cross, the way of Jesus.

There are continuing tensions for me, especially in my work as a probation officer when I act as an agent of the State. On entering social work training I accepted that I would be exercising power on behalf of the State. However, I now wonder how appropriate it is for a Christian to be exercising that kind of power, backed up by threats of punishment. There are aspects of my job that are about bringing people to a realisation that they have acted wrongly and about rebuilding broken relationships. These are kingdom activities.

However, the job of a probation officer also involves enforcing the requirements of the State in a far from perfect criminal justice system. Most of the sixteenth-century Anabaptists recognised that the State had a role to fulfil in a sinful world, but they also counselled that Christians should not involve themselves in exercising its coercive power in order to counter evil. I do not know the answers, although I recognise that my deliberations could result in me leaving my current job. However, I am glad that the Anabaptists have posed the questions. In fact, Anabaptists are distinctive, not just because of the answers that they give, but also because of the questions that they ask in the first place.

The Demonising of the Name "Anabaptist" must be Stopped
Ian Milligan, Glasgow

Ian Milligan lectures in social administration in Glasgow, and is a member of "Bert," a home church/community.

In four words – *The Politics of Jesus* – is how I discovered Anabaptism. Like many others in the mid-1970s, I was hungry for both community and a biblical basis for political engagement. I can't really remember what first took me to the London Mennonite Centre. In the centre I discovered the bookshop and began to read about the Anabaptist story. In fact, on one visit I was browsing in the book cupboard and met John Howard Yoder there. Reaching down a book about Michael Sattler, I asked Yoder's view of it before realising who the author was. John's eyes twinkled, you can imagine.

Basically, what I discovered in reading about the origins of Anabaptism was a wonderful story which, although far in the past, gave me a sense of identity (perhaps romanticised?) and source of continuity. Perhaps my understanding of the gospel wasn't so deviant after all. I discovered that others had been working at this kind of discipleship, counter-cultural and pacifistic, long since. My reading also showed me the flaws of course; it could get extreme, eccentric, introverted, but you had to make allowances for the times and all the persecution.

As a member of a group which calls itself a community, I have taken a particular interest in how the collective dimension of the faith works out. This led to finding out a bit about the Bruderhof and the Amish. None of these groups is particularly attractive to me in terms of the degree of separation and severe morality, and most fundamentally the second-class status of women. But, nevertheless, you can see mighty fine qualities of simplicity, sharing, humility and peaceableness, based on a real commitment to a Jesus-centred faith.

I get the impression that Mennonites are people of deep faith, who are not part of state power structures (and never have been), and who seek to serve rather than be served. Very importantly for me, they don't have typical conservative evangelical hang-ups about evangelism versus social responsibility. That is an inspiration. They seem to have the theological base and discipleship tradition that can maintain an authentic gospel witness in an individualistic, materialistic and violent culture. As someone who lives in such a culture, I find it encouraging to know about the Anabaptist heritage.

Having found out a bit about Anabaptism many years ago, I have often wondered why this tradition had not developed in England or Scotland. I know about the Baptist tradition, but it is pretty clear that it does not have the same style of discipleship that the Anabaptists practised, and there certainly seems to have been no "denominational" tradition of pacifism (in any variant), nor a stress on community. Most early Baptists didn't want anything to do with Anabaptism, despite sharing some of their key theological emphases, such as believers' baptism, voluntarism, higher expectations of the "laity," and so on.

We know this because being Anabaptists is what their opponents accused them of being. The Baptists refused the accusation. The first British Baptists did face considerable opposition from church and state authorities; many were arrested and harassed, and some were executed. But such was the fear and loathing that was conveyed by the term "Anabaptist" that, even during the ferment and turbulence of the early seventeenth century and the English revolution, there was no worse thing you could apparently accuse someone of than being an Anabaptist. Such was the depth of the stigma associated with the word "Anabaptist" that even those who in reality did share something of their theological and ecclesial inspirations wanted nothing to do with them.

How could this have come about? How could the peaceful and blameless lives of these Anabaptists, who simply proclaimed their faith in Jesus, baptised adults and set up their own churches, how could their very name convey terror? Why were these people who helped the poor, refused to take up arms in a most violent century, how could these "little" people be hated so much? I don't really have the answer, although to begin to understand this hate, this loathing, you do have to see the connection with fear.

The Anabaptists struck fear into the hearts of the respectable classes and the authorities because they were a church of the poor. This was a movement which empowered the poor, it made them independent of the rich and powerful. The powers that be could not control them, because they were living by a different base of values and priorities to the rulers of the State, who had long got used to the Church behaving in a way that was acceptable to them.

Thus, although the Anabaptists killed nobody, and in fact were willing to be martyrs, although they did not try and take over the country or rule other people, they were treated as a deadly virus. The educated and powerful used every lie and slander (as well as physical punishments) to stop them, exterminate them and, in fact, more importantly to try to discredit their understanding of faith and practice. These poor people suffered terribly and, while I can see the challenge they posed, it is still very difficult really to understand why they got the depth of hatred piled upon them and their very name which they did. It takes us into the realms of scapegoating and, indeed, the cross.

The bad name of the Anabaptists has nothing to do with the violent uprising in the city of Münster, although it provided a convenient stick to beat them with. Everyone then and every historian since has known that that was not a typical episode and, in fact, was the exception which proved the rule of their non-violent life and witness to the way of Jesus. The fact that historians, church or secular, have chosen to tell us about Münster in the brief mentions they make about Anabaptism when writing of the period is part of the pernicious legacy referred to above. Most historians have been part of the wealthy and secure establishment and reflect the bias to the rich which is revealed when the good news to the poor is made manifest.

This demonising of the name Anabaptist must be stopped, and perhaps that is what is happening now. Although they lived 450 years ago, their genuine attempts at following Jesus must be recognised for what they were: a decent, honest and faithful witness, and brave beyond most of our (British) imaginings. A terrible injustice was done to the first Anabaptists; we need to recognise that and rescue the name, even after all these years.

A Viable "Third Way" which is Truly Radical and Different

Alun Morinan, London

Alun Morinan lectures in the Department of Life Sciences in the University of East London and belongs to a Baptist church.

My initial contact with Anabaptism came just after completing my PhD in the Department of Pharmacology at University College Galway (UCG) in December 1978. As secretary of the UCG Student Christian Movement, I had arranged for a South African-born Mennonite, who had studied in Belfast but at that time lived in Dublin, to speak at one of our public meetings held on the university campus. I cannot remember the exact title of the talk, but it was something on the theme of Christianity and the State. I do, however, recall one point in the talk when he said how he was particularly angered by the display of military regimental flags in some churches, a practice he considered totally incompatible with the Prince of Peace. At that meeting I bought a copy of John Howard Yoder's *The Politics of Jesus*, prescribed reading for every Anabaptist. I returned to England the following year, about the same time as a Mennonite Church was being established in north Dublin.

In 1990 I renewed my contact with Anabaptism when I approached a Mennonite contact about the possibility of his speaking at a public meeting to be organised by my local Campaign for Nuclear Disarmament (CND) in south-east London. One week before the Gulf War ceasefire was announced, he spoke to the Beckenham and Penge CND on the subject of "Taking a Non-Violent Attitude into our Lifestyle." Later that year, I attended my first *Cross-Currents* seminar on Anabaptism at the London Mennonite Centre, and since then have participated in many more, as well as being an active member of the South London Anabaptist Network study group and writing for *Anabaptism Today*.

One of my concerns as a Christian, and what is often most evident among conservative Evangelicals, is a focus on conversion, i.e. the start of the Christian life, which can almost ignore discipleship, i.e. the continuation of it. So the incarnation, death and resurrection of Jesus are preached, but less attention is paid to what happened in between – Jesus' earthly ministry as the model for how his followers should live. Of course, salvation is essential, but that is only the start of our journey, and I believe that discipleship – following after Jesus – and what it means to us, needs to be emphasised much more. "Liberal" Christians tend to another extreme by manipulating Jesus to fit a particular (left-wing) political agenda and calling for society (or more particularly the government) to repent, while ignoring the needs of the individual. Jesus then eventually becomes redundant as their concerns to impress secular revolutionaries begin to take over. As a former card-carrying member of the Communist Party of Great Britain, I have seen the pitfalls in this position.

Where Anabaptism has been particularly helpful is in showing me the possibility of a viable "third way," which is truly radical and different. The early Anabaptists were gathered communities of believers who voluntarily chose to become Jesus' disciples. They maintained a separation from the State (which does not mean that Christians must be apolitical, rather they should not necessarily be linked to a particular political party or form of government) and therefore did not expect any preferential treatment from it. Perhaps most significantly in following Jesus, they adopted his life of non-violence and enemy love, a characteristic very much absent from the sixteenth-century Church and also, sadly so, at the end of the second millennium.

Too often in our individual churches we can feel isolated from others with similar concerns, a view often expressed during discussions in which I have participated at *Cross-Currents* and our Anabaptist Network study group. However, the fact that there are individuals in different churches of various denominations who find Anabaptist ideas so stimulating should be regarded as a strength rather than a weakness. There is no ideal church – and I do not think that even an Anabaptist one would be ideal. After all, what is really exciting and has had the greatest impact on me is not that the early Anabaptists had discovered a new set of ideas, but rather that they had rediscovered something neglected for several centuries previously – what it really means to be a Christian.

Christians are members of an alternative society, a counter-culture we call the kingdom of God. Membership is open to all regardless of nationality, ethnicity, gender, social or economic status; but to make people want to join up, they have to be attracted to the radically different lifestyle of its members. Sadly, too often the life of the Church is a pale imitation of the secular society which surrounds it, with the only obvious difference being a number of "Do Not" instructions on personal morality. While this is all we have to offer, the Church will largely be ignored, but if we discover with the Anabaptists what it really means to follow Jesus, then we will have a major impact on society. And that is exciting.

Anabaptist Homecoming
Noel Moules, Sheffield

Noel Moules is pro-gramme co-ordinator and primary teacher for Workshop, a Christian discipleship and leader-ship training course.

I only met Anabaptism directly in a later stage of my spiritual journey. For me it has not been the initial inspiration to discover, but rather a homecoming. It has provided a sense of place, identity and a network of friendships.

I was a child of missionary parents, born and brought up in India, in the foothills of the Himalaya, until the age of ten. My whole spiritual environment was interdenominational Protestant. In the mid-1960s I was studying in a bible college in the south-west of England. They were heady days! It is hard to communicate the exciting mood of the time. The charismatic movement had just begun and individuals and local churches were being radicalised. But far beyond that there was an excitement and enthusiasm in the air for truth which I have rarely experienced since among most Christians.

It was early during this period that I was reading Matthew 24 when I was struck by verses 23-27: "Then if anyone says to you, 'Look! Here is the Messiah!' or 'There he is!' – do not believe it. For false messiahs and false prophets will appear and produce great signs and omens, to lead astray, if possible, even the elect. Take note I have told you beforehand. So, if they say to you, 'Look! He is in the wilderness,' do not go out. If they say, 'Look! He is in the inner rooms,' do not believe it. For as the lightning comes from the east and flashes as far as the west, so will be the coming of the Son of Man."

These are not the kind of words one would expect to ignite a dramatic spiritual encounter! Nevertheless, in my case they set me on a journey that has haunted and energised my life ever since!

As I read, the first question that struck me was, "How do you tell the difference between false messiahs and the true Messiah?" The answer seemed clear, that it is to do with their real character and the quality of their message. This inspired me to begin to explore, and become a zealot for, the whole concept of the kingdom of God. And it needs to be said that this was at a time when nobody in local churches talked about the kingdom of God, or if they did it was always viewed as something in the future that was still to come.

My explorations into the kingdom of God led me in turn to ask a second question, "What are its values – what makes it so distinctive?" The pursuit of this question took me into uncharted territory, and to the life changing discovery of the vision of *shalom* – the vision which I believe provides the paradigm, not only for all biblical values, but in fact for all truth. Again it is hard to convey just how radical this kind of discovery and thinking was. Nobody I had ever heard spoke about *shalom*, it was a totally alien concept. As I shared my excitement about the total integration of all things in the person and peace of Jesus, as I discussed its obvious implications for the gospel in non-violence, ecology, community, justice, evangelism, discipleship, eschatology and so very much more, I was told in no uncertain terms that my thinking was nonsense. At the very least, it was eccentric and most probably it was false teaching!

The charismatic experience was personally very significant and precious, a vital ingredient at the heart of my journey of discovery. However, the direction of the movement increasingly gave me cause for concern. Throughout, the 1970s was a lonely time in many ways. These were days of thinking through and, in small ways, trying to experiment with the kingdom of God as the expression of *shalom*. The independent charismatic groups of which I was a part were endlessly discussing what it meant to be "New Testament church," but their framework of thinking was very narrow and limited.

By the end of the 1970s and very beginning of the 1980s, I had begun to discover and reflect upon Anabaptism. However, it was a request to write a chapter "Jesus the Peacemaker" in the Evangelical Peacemakers' book *Decide for Peace* and my subsequent meeting with Mennonites that proved a personal catalyst in my more direct links with the movement. Though inspired by the historic expressions of Anabaptism in Mennonite and Hutterian communities, it was the overall ethos of the movement that attracted me and with which I found identity.

At the heart of everything that I have found within Anabaptism is a framework, an opportunity to be among those who aspire to be radical disciples of Jesus. There is the encouragement to explore and experiment with truth; an excitement about that personal relationship with God which takes us on a journey of ever unfolding discovery towards the ultimate expression of *shalom* in its fulness as it embraces all things in the new heaven and earth. Here is the friendship of God, and the people of God. What more can one ask?! For this I am deeply grateful.

A Tradition which Articulates, Sustains and Develops my Faith
David Nussbaum, Little Chalfont

David Nussbaum is The Finance Director of Oxfam and a member of the King's Church, Amersham.

My Christian roots are in evangelical Methodism. Influenced by a number of people in the youth group I belonged to, I took religious studies as one of my A levels, and chose to include church history. This fired my interest in exploring the Christian traditions to which I found a sense of affiliation. This continued through my first theology degree at Cambridge. In addition, I spent a month at a training course at Ichthus Christian Fellowship. There I learned more about how what Christians believe and do today has been influenced – for better and for worse – by the way theology and practice developed through church history.

I took this further in my second theology degree at Edinburgh. There, I focused on the life and theology of Augustine (of Hippo), and took a course on the Anabaptists. I found that a lot of the more objectionable elements in what has become traditional Christianity were developed in the fourth and fifth centuries, and linked to Augustine. When I finished my Master's degree dissertation, I remember my tutor commenting that this was one of the few pieces of work on Augustine that he had read which was written from an essentially Anabaptist perspective.

The following year, I started studying accountancy in Edinburgh, with a view to working in that field. I went to London a few times for job interviews, and took the opportunity to visit the London Mennonite Centre. I subsequently moved to north London, and began going to what was then the London Mennonite Fellowship, together with Kathy (now my wife). This was a church in which Anabaptist insights and principles were being consciously pursued. Here, then, I was able to develop a living experience of participation in an Anabaptist (in this case Mennonite) church, to complement the theological studying and personal reflection I had done. What Kathy and I found was that we joined a church which, of course, had plenty of difficulties and frustrations, but it also maintained a determination to work at these together and to engage its faith with the world. We were members of the Wood Green Mennonite Church for about ten years, for much of which we were members of the leadership team, until we moved to be nearer where my job was based.

What in Anabaptism has been attractive and helpful to me? I have frequently felt uneasy about aspects of the Christian tradition, especially as found in the Roman Catholic and "mainstream" Protestant churches. So it has been important to find that there have always been Christians – and many of them – who experienced this; that what I believe has always been believed by Christian groups, especially those in various radical traditions, such as the Anabaptists. So while I am happy to identify with other traditions too, Anabaptism is the Christian tradition with which I probably identify more closely.

Several features have been especially significant for me. First, the emphasis on the centrality of Jesus and understanding the Bible through him. This was an example of discovering in Anabaptism a tradition which articulated clearly what I already believed, and so sustained and developed my faith. Second, the emphasis on the role of the Christian community, both in interpreting and applying the Bible, and in helping to guide my (and our) thinking when making major decisions about our lives. (Though I do remember that when we asked the church whether this included family planning decisions, members were clear that this was a case for personal decision!) Finally, the focus on peace – *shalom* – has been a consistent source of challenge to me: not so much in finding war to be inconsistent with the gospel of peace, but in how far that gospel has really penetrated my own internal instincts and reactions.

There must have been some chance that I would have continued further in academic theology, and discovering more about Anabaptism was probably one of the things which led me not to do this. I chose instead to pursue training in something (accountancy) which would enable me to earn a living, support a family, and involve myself in the secular world. This is perhaps a rather unusual way for Anabaptism to have impacted. I remember that, some time after I completed my Master's degree in theology, and was working as an accountant based in London, I was invited to present a paper on Augustine at a Tyndale Fellowship Study Group. One of the criticisms I recall receiving there was that my sort of theology led to withdrawal from the world. Now Anabaptism has indeed led to this sometimes, but it seemed strange to be accused of this by a group of clerics and theology dons while I was working in the commercial world.

I worked for about fifteen years in the commercial sector: in accountancy, in venture capital, and heading up the finance function in manufacturing industry. Without the influence of Anabaptism and a Mennonite church, I might have succumbed more than I perhaps have anyway to the values and mindset that these environments tend to encourage. A couple of years ago, the opportunity arose to make a major job change, to head up the finance function in a large charity. Being able to be free to move out of the lucrative world of the public limited company board director and leave its career prospects was, I think, something of a testimony to the impact of Anabaptism on my life.

We have four children. For me, holding on to the intention to welcome having this number of children in our family has also been supported by the values found in Anabaptism. Indeed, our interest in sometimes enlarging our household by having quite a number of people living with us (one at a time!) for various periods has also echoed the Anabaptist tradition, and some of them have been Mennonites too.

I am hopeful and confident that the impact has not finished yet: there is more to come.

Anabaptiste – Moi?
Meic Pearse, Northwood

Meic Pearse teaches church history at London Bible College and at the Evangelical Theological Seminary, Osijek, Croatia, and is a member of the King's Church, Amersham.

My first few meetings with the Anabaptist Network prompted mixed emotions. On the one hand, there was the joy of finding like-minded others: people who appreciated the importance of the Anabaptist legacy; brethren and sisters who could see that Christendom was a Bad Idea; a smattering, even, of those who knew that that wretched man from the town with a name like "Rhinoceros" (or something) had been a Bad Theologian. And now I had the reassurance of knowing that I was not the only one to suspect these things.

On the other hand, there was the realisation of how different we all were. Many of them were not like me at all. Some of them were "ethnic" Anabaptists: people who had family links with Mennonite or Hutterite communities and spoke fluent German with that same mixture of affection and rueful irony as did mid-century Jewish refugees. I mean, I spoke it too but, then, that's A levels and a year in a German Teflon factory for you. Then there were the Baptist ministers in quest of a romantic heritage, for whom the name of John Smyth (even with a "y") was simply too ordinary. Not me, squire, I was on the house-church fringes, and we really were born yesterday.

Next came the lefties, for whom radical Christianity might or might not be important, but was certainly an excellent way of setting a Christian tune to words that were really (I mean really) secular – Falwell's *alter ego*. All that common property and pacifism in the sixteenth century was just so "right on." But I was right off.

So why was I there at all? I'm from a non-Christian background, converted as a young adult, and spent most of my Christian life in an independent church that had its origins as a sort of "Brethren heresy." Swansea is thick with gospel halls: our "meeting" had the same ethos but without the silly rules. As charismaticism took hold of us in the late 1970s, we became a sort of Adullam's cave for Brethren (and, indeed, sistren) who'd received the right boot of fellowship for speaking in tongues or who simply felt that thunderbolts were, on the whole, an unlikely consequence of allowing women to pray out loud in the meetings. Like many another such den of iniquity in those days, we grew fast.

And as we grew, we argued. Sometimes the arguments could get fierce, but mostly they welded us closer together, as we sensed that we were involved in building something very special. By the late 1980s, our identity was clearly with the more radical wing of the house churches. And they, of course, may not have been in search of a theology, but they sure were in need of one. Anabaptism simply described the place to which God had brought us, and showed us why that made sense.

To my mind, at least, Anabaptism was the logical conclusion of a hard-nosed evangelicalism. Seen in that light, there just seemed to be no point in preaching one moment the need to repent and have faith **OR ELSE** (though mostly we put it much more nicely than that), and then turning around the next moment and saying, in effect, that this was merely the tradition of "our wing of the church!" If a Christian was what evangelicalism said it was, then that had implications for how we defined "church." The first thing a non-Christian needed to know was that they were a non-Christian, and we did them no favours by playing along with their delusions to the contrary. The sixteenth-century Anabaptists seemed to me to have had a hold on that simple logic, and had a theology consistent with it. The reason, I increasingly saw, that most modern Evangelicals spoke out of both corners of their mouths at once about the Church was that, although they had an evangelical soteriology, the rest of their theology was borrowed from "Christendom" models that told them about unconditional covenants, invisible churches and Christian countries. No wonder they were confused!

As a church historian, first by hobby, then as a student, and now as a (hushed tones, please!) "professional," I came to see how this state of affairs had come about, and also how different doctrines were worked out in practice over centuries (history being the closest thing we have to a lab test for ideas). That study reinforced my convictions that: a) Anabaptist theology was one of the nearest stabs at replicating early church thinking ever made, while its rivals were mostly theologisations of grabbing political power; and b) Anabaptism represented the most tolerably consistent way of working out essential evangelical insights into everyday life.

I doubt my character will ever be as mellow as the "ethnics;"my credulity will never stretch to romantic heritages; I will never be politically "right on." Ever. And yet, with the passing of the years, the Anabaptist insights about the centrality of discipleship are having a greater influence and impact on my own thinking and perhaps even (ask my wife) upon me.

An Armchair Anabaptist: A Contradiction in Terms?
John Phelp, Bradford

John Phelp is a former agricultural chemist who has been a member of a Pentecostal church for twenty-five years, and is interested in church growth and organisation.

In 1968, I knew nothing of Anabaptists except as a footnote in a book on church history and did not know that they still existed as a living movement.

After years of pondering the matter as a result of contact with Christian Brethren in London, I became a "literal" Anabaptist and was rebaptised by immersion as a believer having been "baptised" as an adult unbeliever. This occurred in the context of a Pentecostal church in Canada in 1970. In effect I'd left the Anglican Church. In the congregation as witnesses were two Mennonites.

In 1968, I left Leeds University to study further in Montreal. In November, I arrived there and soon there was snow, snow and more snow. It wouldn't surprise me if it was in a snowstorm that I was introduced to Arnie and Betty Mae, a young Mennonite couple from Swift Current in Saskatchewan. I was introduced to them by a fellow European, a Frieslander (Netherlands). He was busily kicking over every fence in sight put round him by his religious upbringing. He used to hold parties at which he, I and a Canadian of Scots ancestry and Jamaican accent would retire to the kitchen and talk of higher things.

Arnie and Betty Mae were very friendly to me. We shared times of prayer, Bible reading and reading of books like *Breaking the Wineskins* and *Lord of the Rings*. My memories are of cool drinks on warm evenings, the sound of insects. For many years I thought that one of their favourite eats – lasagne – was an item of Mennonite cuisine. I gathered that Mennonites had a stirring history involving persecution and worldwide migration, ending in Canada and the USA. It was also apparent that they were pacifists and shared a strong sense of common identity. I learned that people I knew with names like Schenk and Warkentin from Saskatchewan were probably of Mennonite ancestry.

Since schooldays I have always been in some way a pacifist, even before any Christian connections developed. I guess that for many years I was quite muddled about this issue. In recent years I've become more interested in such things as conflict resolution, but I admit in a rather theoretical way. I think these ideas aren't very well integrated into my practice. I notice quite the reverse in the story of Dirk Willems of Asperen.

In the late-1980s I had been inspired by Jacky Pullinger's book, *Chasing the Dragon*, and her integration of healing, evangelism and social action. This led me on to such questions as "How should churches be?" "What counts as a successful church?" This has led to a pilgrimage literally and metaphorically. In 1990, I decided to make contact with the Jesus Army with their sympathy toward Anabaptism and to find Mennonites in England. I knew from Arnie and Betty Mae that Mennonites had lived in North London about 1970, but North London is a big place!

In 1993, I took what one Mennonite described as a pilgrimage to some areas of the USA with significant Mennonite connections. Evangelicals aren't known for going on pilgrimages so it seemed a bit odd at the time. It no longer bothers me. I might describe myself as an Anabaptist or "a revisionist charismatic" with its conscious allusion to Marxist terminology.

I'm still on a pilgrimage. I'm interested in the diversity of churches – not some model pressed out by a cookie cutter. I'm more interested in what unites than what makes Christians different. Perhaps in some ways that's a reversal of traditional evangelical concerns with doctrinal purity. As I grope forward, I might say that a sound motivation is worth more than intellectual orthodoxy. An Old Testament scholar once lectured in Bradford Cathedral and all I remember was that he said it was not only important to believe that the Psalms are true but that we would be transformed by putting them into practice.

I grapple with contemporary Mennonites' unity yet diversity, high creativity yet with a long conservative yet paradoxically radical tradition, its humanity yet having no condescension to mankind's rebelliousness against God. I wonder at their seeming addiction to surveying and enumerating themselves.

Finally here's a question: Is an armchair Anabaptist a contradiction in terms?

Shalom   Outworkings
Alison Phelps, Leeds

Alison Phelps is Pastoral Worker of Harehills Lane Baptist Church, Leeds.

My introduction to Anabaptist thinking began in the early 1980s through involvement with *Aslan*, a small Leeds justice charity. It invited members of the Mennonite Centre in London to speak at a memorable day conference on "Living Towards a Vision" – fitting worship, peace, action, lifestyle, community, justice and prayer together biblically. Our own pilgrimage had already led us to share a house with another family, to move from a city-centre Anglican church to a local Baptist church, to value our inner-city surroundings, to protest at the local American intelligence base, to read Ron Sider and Donald Kraybill, to belong to a food co-op, to share vehicles, and to distrust the educational, health and justice systems (hippies or what?!). But listening to these Anabaptists gave a biblical structure and pattern to the disparate elements of our life.

The first attraction was not to Anabaptist ideas in themselves but what we perceived to be a passionate and realistic hunger for *shalom* here and now, motivated by a big vision of the Kingdom. In between being a self-employed graphic designer, community teacher, and parenting Anna and Barny, over about sixteen years and a good few mealtime conversations, *Workshop* weekends, conferences and books, we have understood a bit more about our own roots and heresies. Gradually, a sense of broader Christian history from an Anabaptist perspective has deepened understanding, replaced some anger and stimulated action (in our better moments). Without some sense of being part of a wider Christian community, historically and geographically, the trials and pressures of the local Christian church might have been devastating.

Two months after the "Living Towards a Vision" conference, we started a *shalom* group at church. It met for just two years, but contributed profoundly important ideas on giving, race, youth, unemployment, housing and loneliness, which led to a playgroup, employing a youth worker, an advice team, hostel, holiday clubs and further research. Building in Bosnia and the Jubilee 2000 campaign are more recent *shalom* outworkings. There are a variety of theological strands in our church, and our loyalty to it has sometimes been stretched to breaking point as we have increasingly valued Anabaptist input and tried to share it. Not everyone has been as excited as we are by different ways of thinking. How can we be in a church that still does not value women wholeheartedly, cannot look at economic injustice within the fellowship? And as we reflect on enemy loving, community, and reconciliation, how can we not be?

Having said that, Bill (my husband) is keen to point out that we're not Anabaptists (or Baptists for that matter) and have no intention of becoming such. The only label we embrace wholeheartedly is "Christian" – at least, that's the theory!

More than an Intellectual Journey
Lloyd Pietersen, Bristol

Lloyd Pietersen is an accountant, a Bible teacher, and a PhD candidate in New Testament Studies in the University of Sheffield.

I think I have been a closet Anabaptist for almost the whole of my Christian life. I was attracted to the house church movement in the early 1970s primarily because house churches were concerned about radical discipleship, honesty and openness in relationships, living an alternative lifestyle and community. I have always been sensitive to the contemporary Church's seeming captivity to the surrounding culture and many times found myself wondering whether the Church in Britain would find itself persecuted if Christians truly lived like Jesus. Nevertheless, I would not have described myself as an Anabaptist, as my only experience of the term at that time was anecdotal evidence of strange North American Mennonites and the film *The Witness*, with its portrayal of Amish life.

In the mid-1980s, I read two books which profoundly influenced my life. Jim Wallis' *The Call to Conversion* articulated what I had instinctively felt for some time – that conversion is not just a matter of personal, private decision for Christ, but involves every sphere of human existence, including the social and political. John Howard Yoder's *The Politics of Jesus* helped me see in a new way how central Jesus is for a contemporary Christian social ethic. In particular, his chapter on "Christ and Power" gripped me and led me on a journey, through which I came to be highly critical of much current charismatic praxis in the realm of so-called "spiritual warfare." At around the same time, I preached a series on the Servant Songs of Isaiah in my home church and could not get away from the centrality of justice for the Servant (e.g. Isaiah 42:1-4).

This was by no means just an intellectual journey. My wife and I began to discuss how we could effectively begin to live out the demands of Jesus. For us, it meant at that time saying "no" to the pressure with a growing family to get a bigger mortgage and a bigger house. In fact, we moved from our delightful four-bedroomed detached house into a much smaller and cheaper three bedroomed semi in order to be mortgage-free and to explore the possibilities of a simpler debt-free lifestyle. That was an important phase in our life. It was our way of saying we wanted to demonstrate faithfulness to Christ in a practical way. I am not saying for one minute that this is meant to be normative. At the time of writing we have two houses and two mortgages!

Two other strands are important in my Anabaptist journey. My brother-in-law had been on one of the *Workshop* courses and regularly spoke to me about non-violence as a Christian way of life. What struck me was his personal commitment to non-violence, despite being by nature a pretty aggressive person. This was definitely a lifestyle choice for him – it did not come easily – and has subsequently led him and his family to sacrificial service among refugees in many of the world's war zones. His commitment to non-violence as a way of life spoke volumes to me. Finally, conversations with friends with whom I was involved on the steering group of the New Churches' Theological Forum, convinced me that I was indeed happy to be called an Anabaptist. When I heard about the possibility of an Anabaptist network, I eagerly signed up to be on the mailing list.

Since then, I have had the privilege of meeting many Anabaptists, whose simple lifestyle and radical commitment to Jesus remain a constant challenge to me. Through the network I have discovered the stories and writings of the early Anabaptists. The story of Dirk Willems is particularly significant for me. I long to develop that depth of spirituality which enabled that man instinctively to turn and rescue the thief-catcher at the cost of his own life.

Connecting Radical Church Life
to the Riches of the Past
Ian Randall, London

Photo not available.

Ian Randall is College Chaplain and Tutor in Church History and Spirituality, and director of the MTh in Baptist and Anabaptist Studies, Spurgeon's College, London.

My first encounter with the stories of the Anabaptists took place in the early 1970s. I was at that time assisting with the production of a Calvinistic Baptist magazine, *Reformation Today*, which devoted considerable space to Baptist history. The study of Baptist roots and the relevance of early Baptist life for the later twentieth century were major interests of mine, and these led naturally to an examination of the Anabaptists. I was particularly impressed by the personalities and the thinking of the Swiss Brethren. Through subsequent visits to some of the Reformation centres in Europe, I have tried to understand more of the impact of the various streams of spirituality which emerged in the sixteenth century.

As well as the reading which I was undertaking in the 1970s, my wife and I got to know two Mennonites in that period. The stimulus of friendship with them, which has continued through the years, has been significant. Through them, I came to know of the London Mennonite Centre, and that has proved to be an important resource. I have occasionally made use of its excellent historical holdings and have also been indebted to those based at the centre, who have been willing to give their time to share Anabaptist perspectives with the wider Church.

Much of my own historical research and writing, before and after joining the staff at Spurgeon's College, London, has been on various movements of evangelical spirituality present in England in the nineteenth and twentieth centuries. But I have continued to look out for signs of sixteenth-century Anabaptist insights and influences coming through the centuries. Most recently, I have been fascinated by the way in which Ernest Payne, a leading English Baptist statesman of this century, was affected by Anabaptism.

Here at Spurgeon's College, we have launched an MTh in Baptist and Anabaptist Studies. The course offers, we believe, a unique opportunity for those who wish to pursue postgraduate study in this area. It looks at such issues as the Bible and the creeds, ecclesiology and society. One advantage of the course is that it is available in a variety of modes. It can be undertaken by attendance at college – either full-time or part-time – for seminars, or can be pursued by distance learning.

The vision we have is for careful historical work on Baptist and Anabaptist experiences to be accompanied by contemporary reflection. One of my own concerns is to explore ways in which Baptist/evangelical spirituality and mission-oriented social involvement can be renewed through the wisdom, stimulus and challenge of past experience and of tradition. It seems to me that too many contemporary expressions of supposedly radical church life become rather shallow because they are cut off from the riches of the past. So my comments about the value of the MTh course should not be seen as blatant commercialism, but rather as testimony!

Resisting the Prevailing Social Climate
David and Angela Richardson, Hackney, London

David Richardson is pastor of the Frampton Park Baptist Church, Hackney, London; Angela Richardson is an artist and teacher.

Angela and I both grew up in strong, committed Christian homes, Anglican and Baptist, and both made personal responses to the call of Christ in our early years. As we began our married life at the beginning of the 1970s, we threw ourselves into the youth work of our local Baptist church and began to experience the delights and frustrations of sharing our home with people who would come any time, day or night!

We were determined to apply Christian teaching and values to every part of life and were sometimes frustrated with the warm, personal piety of our traditions that seemed to lack the distinctiveness of the Christian lifestyle witnessed in the New Testament, and at different times and places in church history. We were looking for something that would not be content to accommodate the prevailing social climate so easily.

There were many influences on us in those days: Arthur Blessitt, *Come Together*, and the early groupings associated with charismatic renewal. Then, responding to a call to pastoral ministry and moving to Bradford, we began to explore practical ways we could express the values of the gospel. John Howard Yoder's book *The Politics of Jesus* and Don Kraybill's *The Upside-Down Kingdom* were very helpful. So also were a conference in Leeds, the Mennonite Cookbook(!), the writings of Richard Foster, and meeting Mennonite friends at a time when we were finding ways of coping with our extended family. All of these things helped to bring us into contact with elements of the Radical Reformation that seemed to articulate a vision of a life of practical discipleship, and of a more communitarian approach to church life.

A second pastorate in rural North Bedfordshire only served to strengthen these concerns. Joining an Anabaptist Network study group was an important way of keeping the challenges before us, and we tried to struggle against the demands of consumerism and individualism that so affect the way we read the Bible and hear and receive the gospel in our culture.

Having recently moved to inner London to a small church in a multiracial area, we can see the relevance of all our experience so far and are beginning to articulate a vision for a community of Christians committed to living out the gospel in this area. We see the insights of Anabaptism in the areas of peace and justice, living as a community and practical discipleship as a vital part of our work, and we look to others with a similar vision for help and encouragement. We still feel that we are at the beginning of a journey, and we trust that we will continue to draw strength from the radical reformation tradition for the task of being church in our post-Christian society.

A Pattern of Christian Discipleship Shared by Thousands
Chris Rowland, Oxford

Christopher Rowland is Dean Ireland Professor of New Testament Exegesis, Oxford University, and an Anglican priest.

It was the early part of 1987, and I was in the middle of doing the preparatory reading for a book entitled *Radical Christianity*. It was a chance conversation with a Baptist friend of mine, who was then training for the ministry at Spurgeon's College. I was telling her about my interest in sixteenth-century Anabaptism and she said, "You ought to meet two friends of mine in London." To cut a long story short, later that year I journeyed to the London Mennonite Centre and met twentieth-century Anabaptists, discovering (I have to admit) that this was not a phenomenon confined to the pages of church history books but a real living Christian practice. It was a great discovery, both for my own research and writing (I found myself making links between Latin American liberation theology and Anabaptism), but, more importantly, for myself as I grew as a disciple of Jesus Christ.

Before writing the book, my knowledge of Anabaptism had been the rather dismissive references in the Church of England's Thirty Nine Articles of Religion, and such slight references as might be included in the standard books on the Reformation. That year, I made friends who have sustained me and guided me, and discovered that a pattern of Christian discipleship, which for such a long time I had thought no one shared with me, was in fact shared by thousands of others around the world too. I realised that my inchoate commitment to pacifism, an egalitarian church structure and approach to biblical wisdom were part of other Christians' vision of discipleship then and now. Here were people who thought that the aphorisms of Jesus in the Sermon on the Mount were meant to inform and influence life in the contemporary world (I recall being reprimanded in my student Bible study group for entertaining such views). They were people who were not only committed to peace but to the means whereby it could be implemented, who had a healthy suspicion of the State and its ideology, and who gave a high priority to practical discipleship in the understanding of the Christian faith. Theologically and spiritually, I had found a home in the twentieth century. I no longer had to be a spiritual exile who could only look back to the ideas of Diggers and Anabaptists of yesteryear but as I could find them today, informing theology and contemporary commitments to justice and peace.

Although I have always been an Anglican, I find myself on the edges of contemporary Anglicanism, uneasy with its Erastianism, unhappy about its antipathy to enthusiasm, particularly when it comes to matters of justice and peace. I have found my spiritual home in the Anabaptist traditions. I think it is a spirituality, a way of being Christian, which may (just about!) be practised as part of any church; that is not to say that it is easy to do outside a Mennonite environment. Of course, we cannot put the clock back and get back to the pre-Constantinian situation. What we can do is to recover that sense of Christianity being an alternative culture which characterised the early Christians' understanding of the relationship between the City of God and the human city. I thank God for contemporary Anabaptist churches whose members down the centuries, often in difficult and costly and situations, have kept that vision and practice alive.

The Church as a "City on a Hill" Made Sense
Trevor Saxby, Milton Keynes

Trevor Saxby is a Senior Leader in the Jesus Fellowship (Jesus Army), who leads the Milton Keynes house of the New Creation Christian Community.

I was in my final year as a modern languages student at Oxford. I had been a committed Christian for three years, member of a lively evangelical church, my future pretty much assured. Yet inside, turmoil. God had been challenging me on many points of my faith. Only one thing was certain: the thought of getting a normal "nine-to-five" job, nice house and car, and my faith eroding through boredom, horrified me. It had to be 100 per cent, red-hot, radical discipleship of Jesus Christ, or not at all.

Other questions plagued me. When would I at last be able to read the New Testament without feeling guilty? Why didn't I (or any other Christians I knew) renounce everything to follow Christ? What made St. Francis and people like him throw away everything that most people were desperate to have, and live in simplicity with his brothers? Also, where were accountability and genuine care for one another's souls? And who cared anyway? Why were the hard sayings of Jesus avoided or interpreted away at Christian Union? Where was the power of the kingdom of God that Jesus had promised? Had we all, in "updating" the radical demands of Jesus to our own advantage, shut the door on the miraculous and on genuine brotherly love?

Interviews for the ordained ministry and missionary work brought no inner peace. Then, one day, an inner nudge told me I had to watch a television documentary on the Jesus Fellowship at Bugbrooke Chapel. It certainly wasn't Anglican! Here were people exploring ways of sharing their lives together in holiness and justice for Jesus. It drew me like a magnet.

I visited, and my inner conflicts entered their final phase. In the New Creation Christian Community (the communal living part of the

Fellowship) my heart found home. I had never had dealings at close quarters with ex-convicts, hippies and dope-heads, but here they were, listening to me, smiling at my intellectual intensity, and accepting me as I was. Week by week, God's word of radical separation from the world sliced into my flesh but thrilled me to the core. The Church as a distinct "city on a hill," shining with welcoming light into the dark, searching world, made so much sense. Not living in the world and going to church, but living as the Church and going to the world. A "new society," where love, justice and righteousness dwell!

Yet my heart fought on. This wasn't "safe" Anglicanism – this was dynamite! Was it off-the-rails fanaticism, as so many friends said? Worse, was it cultish? Then to my rescue came the Anabaptists. The pastor began reading from Peter Riedemann's *Confession* and the *Seven Articles* of the Schleitheim Confession. He even asked me, as I am fluent in German, to scour the Bodleian Library for more texts of the Radical Reformation. Weeks of translation followed, but with every page the light shone brighter! With those peasants and artisans of 450 years before, we shared the vision of a godly, non-worldly Church, which nonetheless welcomed all with the gospel without prejudice.

And so it has continued. In common-purse community I have learned to know myself, to face the unlovely things without running, and be helped through them by the care and faithfulness of others. I have been believed in, which brings strength to my foundations. Through receiving sacrificial love, I have learned to give it. Through being a disciple under training, I have learned to be a father to others and to train them. I want, like Paul, to "present everyone mature in Christ."

It hasn't been easy. We've been ripped off countless times, abused and hurt. Yet love never wants to harden its heart. And the joy of seeing many of today's rootless young generation captured by the vision of all-out Christianity, finding home and healing in community, tends to bathe the wounds in our hearts. These twenty years have been a crash course in living with a capital L, and while we in our day are unlikely to be burned, beheaded or have our tongues cut out like many of the Anabaptists, I find that same martyr-spirit at the heart of Christian community. It is the seed of the Church. "For their sake I consecrate myself," said Jesus, and may this ever be our watchword.

Becoming (again) a Follower of Jesus
Martin Scott, Cobham

Martin Scott is director of training for Pioneer.

My first real encounter (having had some less than real ones through "traditional" church history books) with Anabaptism was in the lives of people I respected in the New Church movement who suggested that they were being self-consciously shaped by the Anabaptist movement. Their Christocentric theology challenged me with respect to my reading of Scripture and opened up new possible approaches. The first aspect where this impacted me was on my male bias, having been guilty of seeing Jesus as someone in my own image and making his teaching and life subservient to Paul (or more accurately, my reading of Paul).

Then, over the past six or so years, writings such as *Anabaptism Today* and various books by Anabaptist authors have continued to stimulate my thinking. The attractive element in Anabaptism has been first the emphasis on Jesus – as a result I have sought to become (again) a follower of Jesus rather than simply being a Christian. Having been a Christian for some twenty years I had learned how to pray and read Scripture but was forced to ask whether I could continue to do so without Jesus. Living life in a charismatic community I was challenged as to how Christocentric my experiences of worship were. This same "Jesus emphasis" has also led me to see myself as someone on a journey with valid perspectives but many questions, some of which are the right ones and some not.

Then, in the past two years, the community emphasis that Anabaptists have has led me to a fresh quest as to the nature of church as a community of faith. To bring the influence up to date, with a current expectation of revival, I am being challenged by the Christocentric models of power and exercise of authority. As much as I believe in, and pray for, a genuine revival of Christian faith, I have an (almost) equal level of fear that we will abuse power and will simply look for society to be transformed through legislative power. It is in Jesus that I see the model of the powerful lifting up the broken and downtrodden, and acknowledge that, if I had not come across Anabaptism, other approaches might well have confirmed me in my rightness.

Other movements have influenced me greatly but I can honestly state that, to date, the Anabaptist movement has been the most challenging one to my own paradigms.

A Nagging Ability to Ask Awkward Questions
Martin Scott, Manchester

Martin Scott is a tutor in the Northern Baptist College, Manchester.

My first encounters with Anabaptism were at the very heart of its origins – the city of Zürich, Switzerland. As a Scottish Baptist – and bit of a "rebel" even then – I had been packed off to the Rüschlikon Baptist Seminary to prepare for Baptist ministry. It was a time of extraordinary personal discovery and change, leading to a radical reorientation of my theological outlook and understanding of discipleship.

The Anabaptist tour of the city of Zürich may strike some as entertaining, but for me it stirred anger. Here were people who cared about a sense of community, who wanted an end to hierarchical distinction and who challenged the establishment. Their outlook seemed, by all accounts, the logical conclusion of the work which Zwingli (and others) had begun. Yet their very commitment was their downfall: their honesty and integrity a "fault" rather than a "virtue" in the eyes of those in power. To visit the Wasserkirche, beside which Felix Mantz was drowned, was to visit the death of the ideals of reformation.

Studying the diverse history of the Anabaptist movements in Europe let me see that my early idealism had a certain naiveté to it – but it never quenched the sense of injustice. Nor did it conceal the inspirational truth of the Anabaptist vision of an egalitarian community. Other personal changes – a broadening theological outlook and a radical rethink of gender relationships – took precedence at this point and the Anabaptists went on the back burner.

Over the next few years of ministry in Jarrow and PhD study in Durham, my experiences and study led me again into the area of the Anabaptist vision. In seeing the Johannine community, the subject of my research, as one in which leadership was based not on "office" but on authenticity of discipleship, I felt the history of the Zürich Baptists more keenly. The experience of working in an area where ordinary working-class people had been more or less discarded by a selfish Thatcherite society also stirred some of the instincts which the politics of Anabaptism seem to address.

The move to Manchester in 1990 provided more direct stimulus to develop Anabaptist ways of thinking. Life in the challenging world of the Northern Baptist College was further enriched by the arrival of real Anabaptist people in the persons of two Mennonites. Their acceptance of me, despite my "liberal" theological outlook and tendency toward cynicism about so much of the religious establishment, was a witness to how true Christian love and tolerance can issue in deep friendship and community. In encouraging me to think more deeply about my Anabaptist instincts, they helped me to begin a process of reassessing both my attitudes to people who think differently and my ways of doing things.

Above all this has included a liberation of thought about my area of teaching - namely, the New Testament. I began to notice how much my practice of New Testament study had been influenced by the hierarchical hegemony of western rationalism (phew!). This was a challenge already begun by the encounter with feminist theology, but now it was reinforced from a completely unexpected direction. Why, as a Baptist, was I part of an academy which sought to wrest the Bible from the hands of the people, into which the Reformers had purported to deliver it, and imprison it among "experts?" Surely, if the history of the Zürich Anabaptists teaches us anything, it is a lesson about where the real dangers lie in terms of reading the Bible! It is when the people begin to read and to ask questions of the hierarchy that the shutters come down and the defence mechanisms get into full swing.

The development of a "Ways of Reading the Bible" course in college has allowed me the freedom to work on this issue. Gone is the over-emphasis on historical-critical approaches, and a more balanced attempt is made to encourage would-be ministers to work with the community at reading rather than needing to "control" meaning. A very Anabaptist insight – that the Bible is there to be read in community, by the people of God, in the power of the Spirit of God – has more opportunity to emerge as we listen to the voices from the margins (the poor, ethnic minorities, women) of our still heavily white-patriarchal society. The time has come to do what Zwingli and others decided against in their time – to take the risk of allowing the ordinary people of God to read and to interpret for themselves, to work with the "experts" rather than to be dominated and excluded by them.

In an odd kind of way, though my theological outlook is very much to the "left of centre," I now find myself somewhat in harmony with aspects of the more evangelical communities of the para-church. This has much to do with the encouragement really to listen to what people of different outlooks are saying. It is also, I think, to do with a truly Anabaptist way of living: exercising tolerance, even when we feel most intolerant; co-operating instead of competing. Even if to some others I may appear nearer to Müntzer than to Mantz, I remain deeply grateful to the heritage of Anabaptist radicalism and its nagging ability to ask the awkward questions.

Taking the Bible Seriously and Practising Equality
Ed Sirett, London

Ed Sirett is manager of Make, Do and Mend, a property maintenance business in North London.

I was brought up by parents who were members of a Christadelphian church. I was baptised when I was about fifteen years old. To a large extent Christadelphians believe much the same as many Evangelicals, but since they are (even more) preoccupied with smallest details of doctrine they tend to view all other Christians as very misguided at best. The worship was unvaried in the extreme.

When I was at university, I began to meet other people to whom the Bible was significant; a strange fact since I had been brought up with the idea that no other

Christians took the Bible seriously! Well, after many years, I drifted through much apathy and eventually found myself converted to mainstream Christianity by the people who ran the Greenbelt festival. When I got married and moved to North London, my wife suggested that we could go to the Mennonites – but I was reluctant since I had spent many years escaping from a "cranky little sect."

However, after a few years of attending an evangelical Anglican parish church we were ready for a change; this was due to some problems we were having "fitting in." Both of us like to explore new ideas, not immediately rejecting them but holding them up to the yardstick of Jesus and our own and others' experience. Both of us had significant problems with the clergy/male-dominated leadership which seemed not to acknowledge the talents of many in the congregation. I became somewhat bored with the same choruses being sung repetitively. My wife had significant bouts of depression which made people wary of her and her talents, rather than accepting her as another broken person in the image of God. Finally, we became disenchanted with much of the teaching, which was often simplistic (instead of simply explained) and in a spirit that left one feeling that we were being encouraged to follow Paul rather than Jesus.

On my first visit to the Mennonites I was in tears of relief and joy for most of the service. Here were followers of Jesus, who took the Bible seriously, who visibly practised equality among themselves. The equality was such that it was not something that this community was self-consciously doing, rather it was something so integral to their ways that anyone not doing it would have stood out simply as wrong. This equality was not just between men and women, it was between the young and old, the well and ill (in whatever way), adults and children, and most amazingly between the leadership and the led, those who had been there a long time and newcomers like ourselves.

After I began attending the Mennonite church regularly, I found that many aspects of the gospel which I had suspected were undervalued elsewhere were now held up as central to the teaching of Jesus (such as peace and justice, radical lifestyle changes, mutual submission, the communal nature of decision-making and discerning God, to name a few). Perhaps the most surprising thing that I discovered among the Mennonites was the best aspects of community life that I had experienced in my childhood – but with the merciless god of Sinai replaced with Jesus "full of grace and truth."

Combining Initiative and Creativity with Dependence on God
Jeremy Thomson, London

Jeremy Thomson is a doctoral student in theology at King's College, London.

In 1986, after two curacies in the Anglican Church, I decided that I could not continue within the Church of England. Following a brief career in engineering research and three years' student ministry, I had gone into residential theological training with a vision to build the Church. But, once involved in parish ministry, I discovered that too many conventional activities and expectations prevented me from giving time to what concerned me most – the formation of community as the heart of the Church.

Since various job possibilities failed to materialise, Kath and I left without an income or a home. I decided to spend a year studying biblical interpretation at the London Bible College, and meanwhile Kath spent some difficult months trying to earn an income before finding a new professional direction in teaching hearing-impaired children. My own change of direction came more slowly as I was first unemployed, then working in a bookshop. Eventually, I decided that I needed to do research on the doctrine of the Church and obtain experience and qualifications which would equip me to teach, so I began part-time doctoral research at King's College, London.

In searching for a systematic theological approach to the subject of community, I realised that I needed to find a tradition which made community a priority and which was prepared to question conventional views of authority in the Church. I came across *The Royal Priesthood*, a collection of essays by John H. Yoder, and as I read them became convinced that I had been searching for and now stood within the Anabaptist view of the Church. Since then I have been focusing my research on Yoder's ecclesiology, its fundamental convictions, coherence and importance for all theology.

In the last three years, my time has become increasingly taken up with teaching alongside research. I teach and tutor Old Testament with the Institute for Contemporary Christianity and the Open Theological College, and have been developing an Anabaptist approach in my teaching of students on the Oasis Youth Ministry Training Course in London (Old Testament and Church and Society). I am also a trained relationship counsellor and help to teach a course on counselling skills for Christians.

But an ongoing frustration for me has been the difficulty of finding a church to which I can belong. Kath and I had had some painful and disillusioning experiences in the Anglican Church. We found that reading the Bible and praying together, perhaps with visiting friends, was far closer to what we believed was church life than most of what we encountered in the official churches (superficiality, irrelevancy, introversion, poor preparation and preaching). Are we in danger of holding out for the perfect church (which would, of course, become imperfect once we joined it)?

The problem is not that churches are imperfect, but that most churches experience such community as they have as an incidental accompaniment to meetings (conversations and hospitality occur beyond the confines of most meetings). Church gatherings are commonly held in order to "worship" (although in the Bible, worship is a much broader concept) or to hear "good teaching" but, to most Christians, the idea of meeting to build the church community is novel – yet it lies at the heart of the biblical vision of the church. So when we attend a church service we rarely come across church community, and we come away feeling frustrated at not having encountered much in the way of church as we believe it should be.

The sixteenth-century Anabaptists were not content with church life as a formality; they insisted that the Holy Spirit made possible the vision of the New Testament of a practical, interdependent network of people who might not otherwise have had much to do with each other. I believe that we could learn from them both the joy and the pain of community. In a society shaped by individualism and privatism, churches have the opportunity to provide a contrasting way of life, but only if specific community-building practices are adopted.

Over the years we have attempted to join several local churches – Anglican, Free and Congregational. When we have tried to get to know people, we have sometimes seemed to be viewed with suspicion: is this to do with our past (ex-clergy!)? Unless one is prepared to attend many meetings (and I am already committed for several evenings a week), it seems that joining a church is difficult. Occasionally we have seen glimpses of what a church could be – one which gives community its rightful place. I sometimes think that the only way to see a significant movement in the direction of community is to help lead a church which is prepared to make community a priority, and this would mean radical changes in Sunday gatherings. Is there an existing church that wants to go in this direction?

For me, discovering Anabaptism has been an encouragement: many other Christians before me have faced difficult choices about church allegiance in order to witness to the renewing power of the Holy Spirit in the Church. Discovering the Anabaptist Network has given me hope that there are Christians in Britain prepared to ask difficult questions and make their discipleship radical (I've found that many in the evangelical constituency from which I come are curiously conservative, compared with those in, say, Australia or the US). But I am also more aware of how I no longer fit much English Christianity, how difficult that makes it to find ways to build the Church, how much I must combine initiative and creativity with dependence on God. Anabaptism has renewed the challenge for me of following Jesus.

The Power of Story to Keep Faith Alive
Graham Watkins, London

Graham Watkins is pastor of the Edith Grove Christian Centre, Chelsea, London.

I first discovered Anabaptism as a student Baptist minister in Manchester. As part of the first year, we did a course on "models of ministry," looking at various models and where possible did so using guest speakers. It was the week that two people who have since become friends gave a Mennonite or Anabaptist model, and I left rather confused wondering if I was a Mennonite (confused because this was the first time I had heard either term). I became inspired by the emphasis on community, taking seriously the rights of everybody to interpret the Bible and the importance of peacemaking, social justice and truth-telling. I caught the vision of a movement which demonstrated clearly the way that these emphases are central to the Bible and our understanding of Jesus.

Above all, I also learned the importance and power of story as a major way that the faith is kept alive. This means telling the stories of Jesus and those who followed him, sometimes simply for their own sake. It has meant telling the true stories of Anabaptists who followed the ways of Jesus to their deaths and of learning to tell our own stories. I also found that I could take on these things, call myself a pacifist and boldly proclaim that Christianity has everything to do with politics, without being asked to abandon all that had attracted me to Jesus and all that I had experienced of the Holy Spirit in the process. I had finally found a place where nobody told me that I must choose between things that I held dear (such as the constant pressure to choose between social action and evangelism).

So the meeting of people who accepted the label Anabaptist, which I would now also accept, changed me as a disciple of Jesus, as a theology student and now as a Baptist Minister. The first sermon that I preached using the story of an Anabaptist was on loving our enemies. I used the story of Dirk Willems, who turned on the ice surrounding the village of Asperen in Holland in 1569 to save the life of the thief-catcher who was pursuing him, knowing that it would lead to certain death. In an Anglo-Catholic church (full of people who had not found anything that I had said to them up to this point very inspiring) and before the college tutor who had come to assess my progress as a preacher, I saw the moving power of this story and the importance of seeing the picture which represents the point at which Dirk turned. For me personally this story has become the one that I tell before all others, and to as many people as will hear it, because it reminds us not only that this man took Jesus' teaching so seriously but also that his instant, automatic reaction to turn was the result of virtues or habits learned in the Christian community. Dirk could not possibly have known of the lives and communities he would change when he turned. Recently, I was given the opportunity to visit Asperen, which will remain one of the more moving moments of my life.

If it was only my preaching style that had changed, Dirk Willems might have been quite frustrated with me ("Have I just become a good sermon illustration?!"). Instead, my understanding of being church has changed. I see the importance of becoming a community of true disciples, of being scattered salt and gathered light; neither at the expense of the other. I see the changing of individuals, and the community we call the Church, into something more Christlike as the first step in evangelism, which gives us the right to talk of what Jesus has done for us. I have seen people take seriously the ways and life of Jesus of Nazareth and change in ways which are noticeable to their friends and family who do not know him yet. Finally, having spent years knowing what I do not believe about sharing bread and wine in Communion, I see the positive power of the symbols in speaking of and reminding of the death and resurrection of Jesus Christ. It is the ultimate time to tell the story again and know once more its beauty, pain and power. "Do this in remembrance of me."

Lending Greater Integrity to Being Church
Anne Wilkinson-Hayes, Oxford

Anne Wilkinson-Hayes is pastor of the South Oxford Baptist Church.

Back in the early 1980s, my church in London had links with the London Mennonite Centre, largely through Evangelical Peacemakers, but I'm not sure that, at that time, I ever made the connection that these fascinating people were "Anabaptists." I may have been more wary if I'd known! All I knew about Anabaptists then was that they were a wacky historical sect!

At the Baptist college I attended, I was never much taken with history, and only vaguely engaged with the arguments as to the extent to which Anabaptists were responsible for the emergence of British Baptists. However, on an exchange to Rüschlikon, I remember being very moved looking down into the fast flowing waters of the Limmat under the bridge in Zürich and thinking about the strength of faith that led men, women and children to accept persecution and death rather than recant their beliefs.

It was only later that I realised that Anabaptists were still a living concern. In 1988, HTV invited me to make a television documentary in a series entitled "Pilgrimages." The aim was not to visit classic religious venues, but to enable individuals to make a personal pilgrimage, to uncover the roots of something important to them. I had been very influenced by the writings of Jürgen Moltmann, so we decided to visit him as a part of an exploration of what enables people to resist the dominant ideologies of their time. We called the programme "The Roots of Resistance," and began in a little village near Augsburg which was an Anabaptist community. Here I met Wolfgang Krauss, a Mennonite and a leader of the Church and Peace Movement in Germany. He talked about those early radical communities and related their beliefs to those held by contemporary Anabaptist groupings. We visited the horrors of Dachau together and Wolfgang explained how he met older people on peace rallies, who were now eager to demonstrate and sign petitions. "We did nothing once, and look what happened." I met relatives of those who had stood against Hitler, and I attended various demonstrations against nuclear plants and poison-gas producers. In that brief time, under the gentle tutelage of Wolfgang, I was brought into a whole new way of understanding faith and practice. It was a delight to discover groups who saw peace and justice issues as central to their faith, without sacrificing biblical faith and worship.

The commitment to recovering Anabaptist principles of community, peace and radical lifestyle within my own Baptist tradition has grown over recent years, because these values appear to lend greater integrity to being church. They challenge some of the more triumphalist tendencies, which seek growth and influence. Most importantly, they focus our attention upon the historical Jesus and on his call to do as he did, and this seems critical to the whole future of the Church as we look towards the next millennium.

Rediscovering our Roots
Linda Wilson, Bristol

Linda Wilson is an Associate Tutor at Wesley College, Bristol, and also tutors for various church history correspondence courses. She has been a member of the Bristol Christian Fellowship since the mid 1970s.

It's hard to say exactly how I discovered Anabaptism. I suppose it was through the New Churches' Theological Forum. Because I was interested in church history, I wanted to explore more. I heard about the Anabaptist Network, was interested, and joined the Bristol Study Group.

The attraction of Anabaptism is that it seems to echo so many of the aspects of Christianity which we were trying to engage with in the early years of the house church movement, and which, of course, resonated with early 1970s counter-culture which also influenced us (though we wouldn't have seen that at the time!). So the idea of not being established, of discipleship, of believers' baptism, of Christianity being all-embracing, of comparative informality in worship and in breaking bread, of the importance of relationships and community, covenant – all these things within Anabaptism drew me to it. More recently, as we try to rediscover the important elements of our roots, but with social justice and mission an integral part, once again it seems to speak to us today.

To look at the Anabaptists is to find people in the past who have had a not dissimilar vision, and have often had to pay a great cost to put it into practice. Our attempts seem pale and feeble by comparison! Yet they too were ordinary folk, from whose lives we can learn and take encouragement.

In the local study group we have grappled over a long time now with some of the key issues of discipleship, and, although most of these questions are also under debate within the church (Bristol Christian Fellowship), it is helpful to have a different situation in which to raise them, and the different perspectives that folk from other backgrounds bring. It is a group in which I feel we have developed a degree of trust and openness, at least in some areas, and which I value.

"If I Break Bread with You, I'd Die for You"
Mary Wilson, Taunton

Mary Wilson is a mother and pastor's wife who is active in Halcon Baptist Church, Taunton, Somerset.

My first introduction to Anabaptism was an Anabaptist Network conference held in May 1993 in Manchester. It was like stumbling across real treasure. I had never heard of "Anabaptism" and yet here my insides resonated with what was being said. I was so excited! It was not so much a case of being influenced by, or converted to, a particular way of thinking. Rather, it was a feeling that my spirituality found "form" within the roots of Anabaptism and I could speak openly, worship freely and explore creatively with people of like mind.

Delving back into my life and trying to discern where some of my yearnings came from, I can think only of stories told by my mother. On one occasion as a schoolgirl of eleven, she had forgotten her lunchtime sandwiches. A friend of hers, Miriam, the daughter of a couple in the Salvation Army, said, "Don't worry; come home with me – Mum will feed you." It was immediately after the Second World War and food was tightly rationed, yet when she arrived she was given egg and chips and simply treated as an ordinary member of the family. It had made a lasting impression on my mother and, in turn, I longed for an extended family where sacrificial and practical love was brought into everyday experience.

My experience in taking the *Workshop* course increased my longing for an Anabaptist-like church. I have found its teaching on Church and State, and on peacemaking, etc. very helpful. But actually it was a comment at an introductory session of *Workshop* which made the most impact on me. The course director, talking about communion, said, "If I break bread with you, I'd die for you – simple as that." At the same gathering, reference was made to the church in Rwanda, in which people had been called to do just that. Hutus and Tutsis were told to worship separately. When some refused, saying that first and foremost they were Christian, they were killed. I was learning that at the Lord's Table we not only "proclaim the Lord's death until he comes" (1 Corinthians 11.26); we also proclaim that as a church we are all "one body" (1 Corinthians 10.17) and we reaffirm our commitment to one another.

This call to community ("being saved from aloneness" is another of *Workshop*'s memorable phrases) seems very important to me. Acts 2:42 onwards seems to be a picture of Christian community. Many see this as "unrealistic" – but I feel passionately, along with Anabaptists, that while there can be many different expressions of community – community characterised by sharing, eating together, worshipping and breaking bread – reaching out to include others (evangelism) can be a reality, and should be.

It's so important to be practical. It's strange to me that a people who are criticised as being unrealistic – perhaps idealistic – are especially concerned with making their faith practical. I remember so much of what Mennonite friends have said at times when our paths have crossed; e.g., fill a jar full of porridge oats – a practical (and biblical – Exodus 16) way of remembering God's faithfulness. Or, what will we remember if, in older age, we suffer from Alzheimer's or similar disease? Jingles from *Neighbours* or *Eastenders*? Or what? If we have hidden God's word in our hearts, then when someone recites that portion of the Bible it will stir in our being. How wonderful! So very practical. Not saying "if you love and trust God, it won't happen to you," but saying "should this happen, there will be a way through."

Our church experience in Taunton is one in which we have endeavoured to bring about some of these things. A number of us belong to the local LETS (Local Exchange Training System) group – which gives lots of opportunities to interact doing practical tasks for one another, and which brings us into contact with the wider community. A credit union operates from our church – seeking to protect people from debt and loan sharks. We run a community café on Wednesdays, an opportunity for cheap nutritious food which the fellowship uses as an opportunity to meet together and many people from the estate come in and enjoy (and the local Anglican church come and share in, which has strengthened our links considerably).

We need to grow immensely in the area of "responding to conflict." Being situated on a disadvantaged housing estate, where drug and alcohol abuse is rife, we have had a lot of problems with vandalism, theft, verbal abuse – stones thrown at windows. My husband Andy was "lasered" through a window on one occasion. We need a positive strategy as to how to respond. Sadly, all too often we've reached for the telephone and contacted police, which doesn't seem right somehow – I feel that there must be a way which would enable us to "act out" the gospel to these (mainly young) people.

A Covenant People, Living Kingdom Life Now
John Woffenden, Mexborough

John Woffenden is an administrator of health care for the elderly, and is a leader of the Oxford Road Church, Mexborough, South Yorkshire (Wesleyan Reform).

The first time I heard the name Anabaptism was many years ago, soon after becoming a Christian. Fortunately, it was used in a positive sense, by the pastor of the church where I had become a Christian. Arnold Astwood, influenced by a Quaker, had been a Christian objector to war in the First World War. The term "Anabaptist" had only been used in passing, but in relation to Christians persecuted by Church and State for their beliefs. Arnold Astwood had known something of isolation from both denominational and independent churches. Others, with similar beliefs, had known what it was to support each other in very practical ways when husbands and sometimes wives were in prison for their faith. He had gone on to defend those refusing National Service because they were followers of Jesus. It was at the end of this era that I came into the church that I have been associated with ever since.

This is a church within the Wesleyan Reform Union of Churches. The WRU was formed out of Methodism in the mid-nineteenth century – a move away from the central government of the Methodist Conference. There was the declaration that the Scriptures are the sole authority within the church. Each church within the Connexion would be autonomous with regard to finance and discipline. It was set up as "congregational" with regard to church government. The structure of the denomination would allow for ongoing reform, which comes with better understanding of Scripture. This has resulted in some churches moving away from the tradition of christening, to baptising believers by immersion. Some of the churches within the denomination, including our own, would be regarded as "charismatic." Although it has always been a small denomination, we are seeing a move from the independence of churches to interdependence based on relationship.

Having had a spiritual upbringing in the above environment, real interest in Anabaptism came with its introduction in a study breakfast. We were asking what an Anabaptist meeting might have looked like, particularly with regard to the structure of their meeting. I don't know how well we did, but it did arouse an interest in Anabaptism. Later, some of us would do *Workshop*. A few of us joined the Sheffield Anabaptist Network study group meetings, which were helpful in discovering more about Anabaptism.

Over the years, we have been confronted with the teaching that violence and training in violence is not the way of Jesus or his followers. We were taught that baptism was for believers and should be by immersion. Both of these things have led to conflict, isolation and, to some extent, criticism. At the age of twenty, I refused to do a job at my workplace for the Ministry of Defence, and this ultimately blocked any promotional prospects, a minor inconvenience compared with the suffering of the first Anabaptists. The things that I have mentioned so far – non-violence, baptism, church structure – have all emerged apart from direct Anabaptist influence. Perhaps it should not be a surprise that we seem to have many common links with Anabaptism, because we share a common desire to rediscover our roots, in order to help us to discover what we should be like today. And hopefully, we are led by the same Spirit in our walk with God.

Our interest in Anabaptism has led us to look afresh at the way we handle conflict, the way we understand church leadership, what it means to be a peace (shalom) church, and what it means to be a community of hope. It has been expressed in various practical ways. In the earlier days, interest-free loans were made for young married couples within the church to purchase a house. Some have provided accommodation for people in difficult circumstances by taking them into their own homes. Mortgages have been paid to release people for mission overseas. We try and use conflict, when it occurs, to build us together. We use group hermeneutics to some extent, and give practical support in various ways. We have still a long way to go!

Looking back over the years, there has probably been more Anabaptist influence and connection without knowing it as such. My own family knew Wilf and Nina Wright who had joined the Bruderhof just before the Second World War, and had left with them to go to Paraguay. Arnold Astwood had provided employment for those who had lost their jobs for refusing conscription into military service, or set them up in the fruit and vegetable business. Ron Marsden was one of these, whose brother Jack joined the Bruderhof. It has been a help to some of us to spend a little time at the Darvell Bruderhof. When we encounter various situations we often ask ourselves what they would do at Darvell.

The challenge is to understand what it means to be covenant people, living kingdom life now, in spite of the not-yet. Our desire is to find the empowering presence of God within our midst, for without it we are powerless to be those people.

Thinking and Saying "Subversive" Things
Veronica Zundel, London

Veronica Zundel is a free-lance author and editor who is active in Men, Women and God.

Born to Austrian refugee parents, one Jewish, one Catholic with a Lutheran father, I think I was destined to become a one-woman ecumenical movement from the start! I was brought up with no religion but humanistic socialism; as far as home was concerned, I was "in Christendom but not of it." As a child, I thought Christians believed in an old man in the sky with a long white beard and that this was outdated.

However, I do remember a "sense of the holy" created by the way my father organised Christmas (in the Austrian tradition, on Christmas Eve) with quiet music, real candles on the tree (!) and a bell rung to summon us into the hushed living room. I had something of the same feeling during the Anglo-German carol services we went to at Coventry Cathedral. At about thirteen, I decided to see what my friends had so resented being sent to, and began to go to a Methodist Sunday school. To my surprise, I found the discussions and the stories very stimulating – it was all new to me. Later, I joined a large open youth club at the central Baptist church in Coventry. As I had a crush on the minister, I decided to attend church on Sunday nights as well as club on Saturday nights. He was a remarkable man who, unlike most Evangelicals, preached mainly from the Gospels, and brought issues of social justice into his sermons. I had been "trying out" the idea of God for a while as a response to problems in my family (my brother was suffering from mental illness) and I was strongly drawn to the picture of Jesus presented, feeling "if there is a God, this is what He is like."

When baptismal classes came up I joined, and by the time it came to a decision, I rather hesitantly "took the plunge." I have felt ever since that it was a great privilege not to have been "done" as a child and to have the opportunity to experience full immersion as an adult. Though I had never heard of being "born again," my first thought on coming up was "Now I have started a new life."

I continued in the Baptist church until I went to university four years later; there I first encountered more conservative Evangelicals and also charismatics. I had a powerful "baptism in the Spirit" experience and moved into the Anglican Church, partly because it seemed to be where "renewal" was happening. Anglicanism also appealed to me because of its historical continuity with Catholicism, its liturgy and the beautiful buildings! Also, the parish system seemed to ensure a much greater social mix than I had met in the Baptist church.

However, I think most of my spiritual support came from membership of the Christian Arts Workshop, who seemed to have a much more open attitude and fewer prejudices. My brother's suicide in my final term also made it harder for me to accept the simple certainties of the Oxford Christian Union members.

After university, I arrived in London to work for the magazine publisher who published *Third Way*. This and the Arts Centre Group were major influences in helping me to integrate my heritage of socialism and love of the arts with my Christian faith. At the same time, they both brought me into contact with an evangelical subculture I found continually frustrating and limiting. Settling in Waterloo, I joined and for nearly ten years was a "pillar" of, the local parish church, which was middle-of-the-road, small, very mixed, very inner-city, very accepting, and a refreshing retreat from evangelicalism.

In 1989, I married Ed. *Third Way* was based in Muswell Hill at the time and so Ed and I settled nearby. We had intended to try out several local churches but on our first Sunday we visited an Anglican church in Finchley where I had friends. We liked the atmosphere so much that we stayed four years! But with changes in leadership, it grew gradually more narrow; we were increasingly uncomfortable and in danger of being labelled heretics (I was suspected of introducing "the social gospel" after persuading our home group to do just one study on homelessness).

At last I persuaded Ed to visit the Mennonites, which had always been on our "to try" list. On our first visit we were both in tears, we felt so at home. After a few months of visiting once a month, we left the Anglicans and came home fully. I promptly went into a deep depression, triggered by our failed attempts to conceive, and probably feeling for the first time that I was allowed to break down. The care we received, and the congregation's willingness to use our gifts in spite of my fragility, were wonderful.

Suddenly I was allowed to think and say all the things I had secretly believed for years but which had been labelled as "subversive" in other contexts. I realised I had never been convinced by the triumphalist "let's march on the land, let's recreate a Christian society" stance of so many groups. I had always suspected that Christian action should be grassroots and from a "resident alien" position (I had been an "RA" all my life in any case). Feminism and social concern were here taken as read. No longer did I have to endure the contradictions of infant baptism, or English (not even British), male, public-school culture being confused with Christian lifestyle. Christian teaching, or better still learning, was seen as a process of dialogue, and the Spirit given to the whole body, not just to a privileged few. What joy and freedom! Best of all, Bible interpretation started with Jesus, not Paul; with the Gospels, not the Epistles. Back to where my dear Baptist minister led me all those years ago!

PART II

ESSAYS AND REFLECTIONS

The Return of an Anabaptist Voice:
Listening to the Stories
Chris Rowland

I agreed to write this reflection if a group of us – who meet twice yearly to share matters of concern arising from our Anabaptist convictions – could reflect together on this remarkable collection of stories. As we shared our initial reactions one of our number, amusingly, compared the experience of Anabaptism to the Tardis, the outwardly small and uninviting old police phone box of the TV series, *Dr. Who,* which, once entered, opened out into a spacious haven of sophistication and light. It is an apt description of the experience of all of us. To many, Anabaptism conjures up images of sectarianism and strangeness. For those of us who have been touched by it, it has meant the opening of horizons and a space for our own discipleship which we never thought possible.

All of us are convinced that 1575[1] was a bad year for Christianity in these islands. Although radical "nonconformity" has in various ways produced groups with Anabaptist instincts and practices, that genius of survival and continuity which has led to the indigenisation of the Anabaptist spirit in these islands in the last three decades has been largely absent from the life of the British churches. "Anabaptist" was a name to fear and to reject, part of the sectarian threat beyond the boundary of the Established Church which, according to its *Thirty Nine Articles of Religion,* along with the Church of Rome was to be resisted and rejected. But the themes which emerge again and again in these stories are not narrow or sectarian. *Community, peace* and, above all, the *concentration on Jesus* are Anabaptist preoccupations which are also universal Christian concerns. Each of these is something to reflect on theologically.

The last two hundred years have seen a significant development in biblical theology: concentration on and fascination with the historical Jesus. This is not the place to explore the vicissitudes of that journey of discovery. It is relevant in this context because it matches an important theological instinct which is apparent in these stories and which has characterised similar experiences of Christians down the centuries. It has been vital to try to keep in touch with Jesus. This development took place in academic scholarship by delving behind the pages of the Gospels in search of the "real Jesus." What these stories suggest is something different, an appropriate instinct that the lens through which all life and theology should be viewed is the *story of Jesus*, told in its fourfold way in the pages of the canonical Gospels. It is not the Christ of experience, the rites of church or group, the demands of nation, family or locality – but the disturbing presence of the stranger who met those first disciples by the sea of Galilee and said, "Follow me."

For many, that first resonance was found in a remarkable book by John Howard Yoder, *The Politics of Jesus*, which has for thousands around the world provided a fundamental reorientation in life and attitudes. In my only meeting with Yoder, he said that he was really quite perplexed at the reaction, for what he was doing was merely putting together themes which were already there in the scholarship of the time. That meeting coincided with him reflecting on *The Politics of Jesus* at a seminar in Oxford. The reaction to Yoder that day reflected puzzlement. Whatever the impact of his work on many of us, it was clearly quite marginal to the concerns of mainstream New Testament scholarship. Yoder's concern with Jesus, however, is a deep-seated instinct in Christian radicalism which, to quote Dietrich Bonhoeffer's words relating to the Sermon on the Mount, recognises "the cost of discipleship"[2] and the challenge to lifestyle and attitude which the words of Jesus bring. As a result, martyrdom, peacemaking and discipleship are not optional extras for church people but the very stuff of the Christian life. Experiences of these Anabaptism offers in plenty.

The modern stories themselves are a genre which in important respects continues a theological genre which is characteristic of Anabaptism. The *Martyrs Mirror* and the *Hutterite Chronicle* demonstrate the importance of *story* in maintaining contact with the past, giving a sense of identity to the present, and offering an exemplar of theologising which differs markedly from what has come to characterise the mainstream of Christian theology. The story of Dirk Willems, escaping from capture who turns to rescue his pursuer, has been a formative one for many of us.[3] But all of us will have our particular favourites among those otherwise insignificant men and women who saw in what we now term "Anabaptism" ways of being faithful to Jesus Christ which demanded, literally, their life, their soul, their all. Such collections have ensured that these women and men have some memorial to stand alongside the "famous men" of passages like Sirach 44.

Of course, narratives and anecdotes are the very stuff of the Bible, and so in an important respect there is nothing original in all this. But, as in so much else, what has happened here is a recovery of a dimension of the reflection on the experience of God (which, after all, theology is about), which has got lost among the undergrowth of intellectual sophistication. Now there is a strong anti-intellectualist streak in the Anabaptist story, which one should not ignore. That has weaknesses as well as strengths. Its great strength, however, is that by its resistance to over-elaboration and sophistication it affirms the simplicity and inclusiveness of the theological task. All God's children can be moved by the Spirit to offer insights from the treasure store of God's grace.

Another feature of Anabaptism to which the stories point is a sense of *community*. In different ways and to different extents there has been in many congregations an experience of Christian fellowship as deeply alienating because it has neglected the fundamental precept of 1 John 4.20: "How can you love the God whom you have not seen, if you fail to love the brother and sister whom you have seen." Still, despite the liturgical changes in most mainline churches, the sense of community is either largely absent or is consigned to some kind of extra-curricular activity in occasional home groups. The structures of most ecclesiastical buildings and the activities that go on in them militate against the sense of fellowship and community which are at the heart of the earliest Christian eucharistic worship. Most contemporary churches deal with the lack of a sense of human fellowship by the addition of the optional cup of coffee after the service. But such occasions need to be at the very heart of the eucharist as a sign of love. Ellie Kreider asks, pertinently: "Isn't it possible that a way to renewal of Sunday eucharistic worship could be through reclaiming Jesus' own approaches of love for outsiders, his radical invitations, and his generous table hospitality?"[4] That is not just an "open altar" policy, but a challenge to think about the centrality of human fellowship in a meal and in conversation as being at the heart of Christian worship – a disturbing thought for most contemporary eucharistic practice.

To return to the image of the Tardis for a moment, what many of us have discovered is a positive attitude to our sectarian roots. The usual caricature of a sect as a restricted, impoverished life fails to do justice to the space for human maturing in God which the Anabaptist vision offers. Sectarianism has a negative flavour in Christian circles. We should think again about facing up to our sectarian inheritance, particularly in the experience of the pre-Constantinian Church and the continuities with that which have emerged throughout history, of which various forms of Anabaptism are examples. We should not concede the moral high ground to those who claim to be inclusive and less discriminating in their baptismal practice.

Rites of passage are important and that service offered by a national church is not without its theological propriety. Nevertheless, the sectarianism which we all so much balk at is endemic in the baptism service of every church – more so here than in other acts of worship in the church, the eucharist included. At the heart of the service is a dualistic pattern of thought which accurately encapsulates the notion of transfer from one kind of allegiance to another. Boundaries are set more clearly here than at almost any other moment in Christian worship. The baptisand moves from darkness to light, from the realm of the powers of evil to the realm of God. There is a passage through water, a cleansing, a newness – all effecting a boundary which has to be crossed. In the actions and words of the baptismal liturgy the cost of discipleship is most clearly enunciated.

Such patterns of thought and action are characteristic of groups with clear boundaries. In the sociology of religion the *sect* has been contrasted with the *church*. The latter is the all-embracing body whose boundaries are blurred and which makes it possible for people to be comfortable on the margins with only fragile or nominal commitment. The sect is different, however. It has rules of membership. The boundary between insiders and outsiders is relatively clear. The baptismal service keeps alive the sectarian character of Christianity. Christianity started life as a form of sectarian Judaism, with clearly defined boundaries on the basis of belief and practice. Until the time of Constantine, emerging Christianity was characterised by such a sectarian spirit. The catechumenate (instruction for new believers) was long and thorough, putting to shame our lack of rigour in baptismal preparation. But at the heart of the whole baptismal experience was the clear message of a transfer from one dominion to another, involving the acceptance of Jesus Christ as king of kings and lord of lords.

Even after Christianity became the religion of the state, the rites of initiation have kept alive that sectarian spirit which is of the essence of Christianity, doing justice to which is a central feature of our theological task. For this reason, I wonder whether the Church is right to make the eucharist the exclusive rite and be more all-embracing in its baptismal practice. I can see how a case can be made (notwithstanding the tradition of the Church) for Christian communities offering an open table to which all who wish may be invited to share in the eucharistic fellowship, while reserving the service of baptism for those who wish to be committed to that pattern of life which they glimpse in the fellowship of the eucharist.

The *Martyrs Mirror*, the collection of Anabaptist stories in which we encounter Dirk Willems and the London Anabaptist cell of 1575, offers evidence of an alternative tradition of Christian discipleship. This tradition was formally outlawed in England towards the end of the sixteenth century when the Anabaptists were driven out of the country. In it, and in other texts from the Anabaptist tradition, there is evidence of a pattern of discipleship in which teaching and learning is more *participative*. Stuart Murray of Spurgeon's College has investigated the evidence of early Anabaptist congregational life and concluded that there is evidence of an approach to the interpretation of Scripture which contrasts with that of the Magisterial Reformers. Whether because they could not rely on a permanent leadership because of persecution, or because of a latent anti-clericalism, or out of a sincere conviction, there is much evidence to suggest that the whole congregation was involved in the interpretation of Scripture. A crucial verse often quoted is 1 Corinthians 14:29, which referred to the participation of the congregation in discerning the theological truth of what is being said. Also quoted is Jeremiah 31:33-34 ("They shall all know me from the greatest to the least").

According to Murray, three theological convictions undergird the hermeneutic community: what he describes as "the theologianhood of all believers," the centrality and continuity of the Church in God's purposes and the belief that the gathered church was the main locus of the Spirit's work.[5] Murray recognises that, for a variety of reasons, this model was not always practised, and that the exigencies of persecution and the struggle for survival brought about a less participative practice. Nevertheless, there is sufficient evidence to suggest that their practice provides a challenge to the assumption that "ordinary" readers or hearers of Scripture are hermeneutically incompetent. It is a warning against the danger of relying on experts whose expertise may not be tested in the setting of the congregation. Undergirding it all is the conviction that ordinary believers can be informed by the Spirit, so that their reading will not be simply be a pooling of ignorance. Rather, openness to the Spirit will yield insights that the Spirit enables in any and all, leading to new wisdom and insight and the ability to judge which opinions are erroneous. It represents a hermeneutical option which is based on faith and the grace which God can give, rather than the safety of dependence on received wisdom alone or expert opinion.

This represents a rather different approach to ordinary readers of Scripture as compared, say, with what we find in Calvin's Institutes (IV.3). Here we have a picture of the learned pastor functioning as a teacher to guide his pupils into the ways of truth and guard them against false teaching. An immediate reaction is to say that Calvin is the more realistic in his approach, more open to the ease with which the truth of God can be corrupted. But the early Anabaptist teachers were as aware of this as any. Menno Simons, for example, was a leading figure in trying to enable the survival of the Anabaptist vision after the debacle of Münster and the horrors of a supposedly theocratic regime in that city. For all that, however, he hung on to the conviction that God gives wisdom to ordinary Christians to find in the Scriptures things which might be hidden from the wise and learned. This needs at all times to be subject to the discerning critique of the congregation; indeed, discernment is one of the gifts of the Spirit.

One issue that emerges in the late-twentieth-century British and Irish stories is the emphasis on the indebtedness to *generic* Anabaptism as opposed to the specific manifestations of Anabaptism in the historic continuations of this vision among groups like the Mennonites and the Hutterites. Of course, encounters with either of these two groups is not easy for many people in Britain. There are only two Bruderhof communities and one Mennonite congregation. There is danger in our attachment to Anabaptism as such, particularly of idealisation or romanticism. If there was any difference that emerged in our discussions in the Anabaptist Theological Circle, it was between the denominational Anabaptists and the rest in our group over the need for embodiment of the vision. That there is an issue here there can be no doubt. A fundamental feature, and something which attracted many of the writers of the stories to Anabaptism, is the need for a sense of community in Christian discipleship. That actually happens for many, however, via artificially constructed networks of sympathetic people across several churches, rather than within a particular denomination, which may at times be distinctly hostile to the tenets of Anabaptism.

While it is true that every community is destined to be engaged in a struggle between its ideals and their practical implications, there is always a risk that "spiritual Anabaptists" may be engaged in a kind of nostalgic yearning for something which they do not find in their own churches and which would be impossible to implement in any church. Doubtless many of us, if we lived in North America, might find ourselves worshipping in Mennonite churches. But as that option is not readily available to us here, there is a fall-back strategy of creating networks and study groups to enable the vision and practice to flourish. There is nothing particularly "un-Anabaptist" about this. Indeed, it seems to me to exemplify exactly those strategies for survival in exile which have been so characteristic of Anabaptists down the centuries.

What is more, that option is not a comfortable one. It is clear from the stories that Anabaptism is not a painless hobby which attracts little of the opprobrium of the past, for the discomfort and spiritual struggles which are going on underline the sense of dislocation and the longing to rekindle something which has been lost in British Christianity. Of course, for those who belong to churches with family resemblances to Anabaptist churches (like the Baptists), there is less of a tension than there is for those Episcopalian churches like the Roman Catholics and Anglicans, for whose members there are posed rather pointed issues of conscience over issues like baptism and authority.

In our day, such ecclesiastical issues may not lead any of us to the stake, but this should not diminish the political character of this theological discipline. What was so disturbing about Anabaptists in the sixteenth century was their subversive potential: they challenged the authority of magistrates, the conformity to organised religion, and threatened national security by their refusal to bear arms. The political character of martyrdom is one that Anabaptism shares with pre-Constantinian Christianity. It is not that either they or the early Christians were engaged in a self-conscious kind of political theology. Rather, those whose commonwealth was in heaven simply refused the ultimate authority of earthly rulers, even if they were commanded to pray for kings and princes. The problem in this, as those who wrote the thirty-eighth article of the Church of England realised, is that this can involve questioning the theological propriety of private property: "The riches and goods of Christians are not common, as touching the right, title, and possession of the same, as certain Anabaptists do falsely boast." Nevertheless, the conviction that "the earth is the Lord's and the fulness thereof" (Psalm 24:1) demands of disciples of Jesus a different perspective on property as Acts 2–4 , the emerging monastic movement and countless later Christian groups have borne witness to. Of course, the descendants of the Anabaptists are themselves divided about the pragmatics of private property, but they share a deep-seated suspicion of the right of the individual, family, group or nation to the right of ownership. There is in this a deep-seated political radicalism, which is not a manifestation of the radicalism of late-twentieth-century socialism but a resonance with a fundamental feature of Christian theology down the centuries.

The story of the emergence of Anabaptism and the different traditions which emerged from those inchoate beginnings are stories about brave individuals who maintained networks, supported and enabled scattered communities to maintain a vision of Christian discipleship in times when communication was not facilitated by the electronics of a technological age. One is reminded in all this of the remarkable ministry of Paul and, for me, the parallel situation in contemporary Brazil, where grassroots communities maintain contact by travelling missionaries and letters.

When I last visited the north-east of Brazil, I travelled inland from the large city of Fortaleza, a six-hour bus journey into the interior of Ceará to a town called Sobral. There I met members of a group who called themselves "The Day of the Lord Movement." The movement consisted of a network of communities in the countryside surrounding Sobral. They had been formed as the result of a popular education programme in the 1970s organised by the local Catholic diocese. Since then they had kept themselves in being and had encouraged contacts between the communities. Although initially they had been organised by a local priest, they had become entirely lay-led and manifested many of the characteristics of the *communidades eclesiais de base*, so typical of the Brazilian Roman Catholic Church and the bedrock of liberation theology. At the heart of the individual communities was the church in each of those scattered villages; these communities were visited only occasionally by a priest or religious and were largely left to fend for themselves.

Over the years they had built up a remarkable network of communication based on reciprocal visitations and the exchange of letters. The letters covered a variety of subjects including issues of land rights, victimisation of tenant farmers and the meaning of Scripture and doctrine. I had the chance to look at some of the letters. What was so striking about them was the thoroughly Christian tone of each one, even when mundane issues such as the rights of sugar cane workers were being discussed. As I read the letters and listened to the story of the movement, I was struck by the resemblances between these scattered communities, the Pauline churches of the first century and the Anabaptist churches of the early modern period. Like the Pauline churches, they too had known their splits and suspicions of various leaders and their styles. But above all, they shared their letters. Here, it seemed, in the late twentieth century, without the benefits of technology, communication had to be carried out by more laborious means. The epistolary world of the Pauline Corpus was alive and well, enabling contact, unity of principle and purpose, and throughout creating the space for a very different perspective on life.

When I visited Brazil, the country was in the grip of election fever, which had engulfed even this remote corner of the land. In the face of this, members of the group commented on the process which they were being persuaded to get caught up in: goodies and promises abounded, as did adulation of the candidates by rich and poor alike. How similar, remarked one old man, was this to the graphic picture of the adulation of the Beast in Revelation with the praises of power and influence and the threats to those who would stand aloof! Being part of this alternative network meant in some sense standing aloof, because it had become possible to see things from another perspective, different from that being fed them by the national TV network or the strong men whose job it was to persuade the local peasantry to cast their votes aright. Echoes here of the "counter-cultural" emphasis which is so typical of Anabaptist spirituality.

In some ways their story, like those contained in the *Martyrs Mirror*, is unremarkable. There is little political heroism to tell of or dramatic confrontations with authorities, whether political or ecclesiastical. Yet their story is typical of thousands of small communities in Latin America which are the stuff of liberation theology. There is little political militancy, and yet in the midst of it all there is something distinctive and authentically evangelical about it all. As far as I am concerned, the evocations of the Pauline churches were most striking. They too were little more than a blip on the radar screen of Roman history, scattered groups amounting at most, one suspects, to only a hundred or so persons. The connection between the Pauline churches, the scattered Anabaptist communities and the CEB's of Brazil is one that is not often made.

Such activities should compel us to look afresh at the letters of Paul. Instead of starting with the themes of Romans and Galatians – the Law, righteousness, grace and redemption – perhaps we should start with the activity of the man himself and the churches he founded. If we do, we shall find a story of enormous dedication and energy consisting of two parts. First, there is the community formation in which groups of Jews and pagans were created, nurtured on the basis of reading of the Bible in the light of Jesus Christ. Second, there is the task which occupied the last years of Paul's career: the collection for the poor in Jerusalem. It is that to which he is alluding (probably for the first time in the extant letters) in Galatians 2:10: "all they asked was that we should keep in mind the poor, the very thing I have made it my business to do."

I have dwelt on this as a way of introducing what, I am sure, will be for Alan and Ellie Kreider something which will cause them unease, but which is crucial in any kind of reflection on the stories: their role as Mennonite missionaries in the British Isles over the last twenty-five years or so. Unsurprisingly, their name crops up from time to time in these pages. They have engaged in activities which resemble those of Paul and his companions and of the Sobral movement –

networking, travelling and speaking. Those who know them well will
testify to their labours among us and the miles they have travelled in
the service of the gospel as they have "serviced" small groups up and
down the country by their preaching, pastoral work, insight and human
warmth. Alan's words about evangelism in the early Church which
conclude his justly influential Laing Lecture (given at the London
Bible College in 1995) aptly sum up the character of their missionary
work in these islands and the kinds of issues they have urgently but
gently placed before British Christians during their time here:

> The early Christians . . . ask us some questions. "At work
> or at home," they might well ask us, "are you known to
> your neighbours? Are you known as members of a
> *superstitio*, a deviation from the norms of accepted
> behaviour? Are you distinctive because of Jesus, whose
> teachings and way offer you perspectives and ways of living
> that are new? And how about your congregations? In the
> way that they function and worship, are they becoming
> communities of peace and freedom which are evidences of
> the truth of the gospel? . . . [A]s you prepare people for
> baptism, are you equipping them to live freely in the face
> of the addictions and compulsions of our time? Are you
> teaching them new narratives . . . so that they are being
> re-formed into people who are distinctively Christian?
> Finally in your worship what do your rites... say about
> your churches' beliefs and priorities? Are your rites strong
> and living, enabling you to address the issues that really
> trouble your communities? Do you evaluate your worship
> primarily by how it makes you feel or by the extent to
> which it shapes your character – as communities of faith
> and as individual Christians – so you look like Jesus
> Christ?"[6]

Alan and Ellie will be the first to give God the glory. But for those
of us who have been touched by their ministry we can thank God for
the way in which He has supported and endowed such gentleness
and wisdom to enable the return of an Anabaptist voice to these
islands.

NOTES

[1] For the reasons, see Alan Kreider's chapter, p. 176 ff in this volume.

[2] Dietrich Bonhoeffer, *The Cost of Discipleship* (London: SCM Press, 1948).

[3] This story is told in Thieleman van Bracht, *Martyrs' Mirror* (Scottdale: Herald Press, 1950):741-742. Significantly, reflections on this story have twice appeared in *Anabaptism Today*, in Issues 6 and 15 [eds.].

[4] Eleanor Kreider, *Communion Shapes Character* (Scottdale: Herald Press, 1997):253; *Given for You: A Fresh Look at Communion* (Leicester: Inter-Varsity Press, 1998):224.

[5] Stuart Murray, *Spirit, Discipleship, Community: The Contemporary Significance of Anabaptist Hermeneutics* (PhD Thesis, Open University, 1992):234. See also, Stuart Murray, *Biblical Interpretation in the Anabaptist in the Anabaptist Tradition* (Kitchener, ON: Pandora Press, 2000).

[6] Alan Kreider, "Worship and Evangelism in Pre-Christendom," *Vox Evangelica* 34 (1994):30.

How a Network Works: Reflections on the Development of the Anabaptist Network in the British Isles

Stuart Murray

An Anabaptist Network

The Anabaptist Network in the British Isles was formed in 1992. It currently comprises about 550 people from all over Britain and from a wide range of church backgrounds. Some are simply names on a mailing list, interested in keeping in touch and knowing about activities of the network. Others are much more fully involved in exploring the implications of Anabaptism for discipleship and church life in contemporary culture.

The network sponsors study groups in various parts of the country, which offer opportunities every couple of months for members of the network to meet together informally and locally to explore Anabaptist themes and their contemporary significance. Some groups have met for two or three years before disbanding, feeling that they have achieved their aims; others have continued to meet over several years. Each has developed its own identity and flavour. The East London group has explored the relevance of Anabaptism for inner city mission and ministry. The West Midlands group shares food and eucharist together regularly and has participated together in a protest about world debt. Alan and Eleanor Kreider have visited the groups at least annually, sharing in their discussions, providing resources for study and acting as a human link between the groups.

The network has also organised several conferences. In May 1993, we met in Manchester to reflect on the demise of Christendom in Europe and the implications for the church and its mission. In October that year, we met in an Anglican theological college in Nottingham to learn from the early church and its pre-Christendom witness. March 1994 found us in Bristol at the oldest Baptist college in the country, asking questions about Anabaptism and local church practice. Then in May 1994, we held our first residential conference at the Hutterian Bruderhof in East Sussex. Further conferences took place in Leeds in September 1995 on the theme "Roots for Renewal" and at the Wildfire Community in Worcestershire in April 1996 on "The Joy and Struggle of Creating Community." We returned to Bristol in May 1997 to explore the role of stories in building community and met in the West Midlands in November 1998 to consider the implications of becoming a Peace Church.

The emergence and growth of this network has taken many people by surprise – not least those involved in promoting it! It represents a remarkable surge of interest in Anabaptism in a nation with very little historical connection to the Anabaptist tradition.

Anabaptism in Britain

In October 1993, members of the Anabaptist Network participated in a dialogue with representatives from the Church of England. This was the first formal conversation between Anglicans and Anabaptists since the considerably less friendly exchanges in the sixteenth century. Alan Kreider's chapter in this book is a revised version of a paper he presented on that occasion, telling the story of the few Anabaptist Christians in Britain in the sixteenth century.

Between the sixteenth century and the early twentieth century, despite the almost non-existent presence of Anabaptists in Britain, the fear of Anabaptism remained and was enshrined in the *Thirty Nine Articles* of the Church of England. Throughout this period the term "anabaptist" was used quite freely to castigate radicals and non-conformists, but the limited information we have about these individuals does not support the claim that they held distinctively Anabaptist views. Meic Pearse, a member of the Anabaptist Network and lecturer at London Bible College, who has done doctoral studies on English radicalism, concludes that it is not meaningful to talk about "English Anabaptism" during this period.[1] For most of the past four centuries, Anabaptism has played no part in British church history. Continental Anabaptists had some influence on the development of the English Baptist churches.[2] But most other traditions developed without interaction with Anabaptist ideas. Generations of British church leaders have encountered Anabaptists only as footnotes in history books; most church members have never encountered them at all.

During the past sixty years, however, two communities with historic Anabaptist connections have returned to the United Kingdom: the

Mennonites in North London and the Hutterian Brethren at Robertsbridge in East Sussex. The London Mennonite Centre has been a persistently subversive influence and has played a key role in the emergence of the Anabaptist Network. Through its teaching programme, hospitality, specialist library and Metanoia Book Service, it has provided resources for the study of Anabaptist history and convictions. Its *Cross-Currents* teaching programme has introduced many to radical discipleship, peace, community and the Anabaptist tradition. Participants have returned to their churches with fresh insights and renewed vision. The more recent *Bridge Builders* programme has already become a highly respected resource for those concerned about conflict resolution.

The Hutterian community developed from a Bruderhof which was formed in Germany in 1920 but was ousted in 1937 and came to England. Forced to relocate again as a German-speaking community under suspicion in the war years, the community settled first in Paraguay and then in the United States before returning to England in 1971. During these years the members of the Bruderhof discovered the Hutterian tradition and became associated with this. But until recently these communities were the only congregational expressions of Anabaptism in the United Kingdom.

Many others, though, have been discovering Anabaptist writings and sensing that in Anabaptism are resources for renewal and helpful guidelines for mission and discipleship in post-Christian Britain. A significant influence has been *Workshop*, a leadership and discipleship training programme run by Noel Moules. Over the past 15 years, thousands of Christians from a wide range of churches have found this course, which is thoroughly imbued with Anabaptist values, to be a life-changing and perspective-altering experience. Noel's passion for what he calls "shalom activism" is infectious and we were in no doubt that we should ask him to contribute to this book an essay exploring the heart and soul of Anabaptism in Britain.

Anabaptist values and perspectives have begun to impact Christians from Catholic, Anglican, Quaker, Methodist, Baptist, United Reformed Church, Pentecostal and House Church backgrounds. For a tradition that is often accused of being sectarian, Anabaptism in Britain is remarkably ecumenical. The Anabaptist Network has made visible this growing interest in Anabaptism and has encouraged further exploration.

It has been a rallying point and an opportunity for dialogue. New members joining the network have frequently expressed a sense of "coming home" and relief that they are not the only ones attracted to the Anabaptist tradition and concerned about the issues it raises: in their own churches, few seem interested. They have also been pleased to find that we are a network, not an institution, an informal coalition rather than a movement, and relational rather than denominational.

Anabaptism Today

The breadth of interest, in terms of both people and issues, is apparent from the authors and themes of articles appearing in the network's journal, *Anabaptism Today*. Published three times a year since November 1992, this journal is dedicated to exploring radical church history and its implications for discipleship today. Its aim is to provide resources for those interested in Anabaptism, by introducing readers to sixteenth-century Anabaptists, printing articles that reflect on the significance of Anabaptist convictions for church and society at the threshold of the twenty-first century, and encouraging an ongoing dialogue. Among the authors and themes have been the following:

• Adrian Chatfield was a delegate at the Anglican-Anabaptist meeting. He lectures at an Anglican ministerial training college in Nottingham but so identifies with the Anabaptist tradition that he was unsure which group he was representing. Interviewed in Issue 8 (February 1995), Adrian commented that what appealed to him about the Anabaptists was their willingness to start from scratch and to break down hierarchical patterns in their churches. He described the Anabaptist Network as a "seedbed for renewing the church" and the Anabaptist tradition as uncomfortable and thought-provoking. In common with many network members, Adrian is concerned to draw on other traditions as well as Anabaptism – especially Celtic Christianity.

• Eoin de Bhaldraithe is a Catholic monk at Bolton Abbey in Ireland, who for many years has been a good friend to Mennonites in Ireland. He contributed to Issue 15 (June 1997) an article examining evidence for adult baptism in the early church and in Irish Christianity, concluding that "many of the holy wells in Ireland were the adult baptisteries of the pre-Norman church."

• Roger Forster leads the independent Ichthus Christian Fellowship in London with its almost 2,000 members and is a key figure in the church planting movement in the United Kingdom. In an interview in Issue 7 (October 1994), he recalled his discovery of the Anabaptists as the time when he felt he had "come home." Roger commented that "it was this kind of church life, community experience, love and non-violence that deep down I was longing for." Roger's influence as a teacher within the House Church movement means that many others in that network of churches have been encouraged to explore the Anabaptist heritage.

• Nigel Wright is senior minister of a large Baptist church near Manchester, an evangelical charismatic theologian, preacher and author whose doctoral thesis explored issues of church and state in dialogue with John Howard Yoder and Jürgen Moltmann. He wrote a three-part article on this theme in Issues 7-9 (October 1994-June 1995), but also contributed a more personal reflection on the impact of Anabaptism on him in Issue 1 (November 1992). Here he described the emergence of sixteenth-century Anabaptism as a "magic moment, a breaking in of illumination through the hard crust of resistant humanity" and recalled a visit to the site of Felix Mantz' martyrdom in Zürich, where "I felt myself to be at a place of breakthrough." He concluded that "the church ecumenical might benefit from the leaven of Anabaptist thought as it relates to responsible discipleship, the believers' church, and freedom of the church from dominance by state and culture . . . the motive for renewed interest in Anabaptism is not narrow sectarianism, but ecumenism in the belief that illumination is here for us all."

• Judith Gardiner is a part-time early church historian, Mennonite church member and local politician who lives in inner London and is concerned with issues of justice in society and the church, including partnership between women and men. Writing in Issue 7 (October 1994) about Anabaptists in the political realm, Judith argued that their historic stance of separation does not necessarily mean disengagement from political involvement. Biblical principles might be worked out in different ways in the sixteenth and twentieth centuries.

• Harry Sprange is a Scottish Baptist minister, who runs an extensive children's ministry called Kingdom Kids. He has written a book on the role of children in Scottish revivals and contributed an article in Issue 6

(June 1994) about children in the Anabaptist tradition, expressing concern that "few of those committed to a concept of church as a voluntary association of believers have grappled fully with how children fit into this understanding." We have tried to encourage critical reflection on the Anabaptist tradition, as well as appreciation of its heritage, and we are grateful to Harry and other writers for challenging us on such issues.

• Trevor Saxby is a leader within the Jesus Army, a radical charismatic movement whose members practise community of goods, evangelise effectively among homeless people and drug addicts, and wear army-style jackets (in the tradition of the Salvation Army) to symbolise their membership of the army of God and their commitment to spiritual warfare. Interviewed in Issue 5 (February 1994), he explained how discovering Anabaptism and especially the Schleitheim Confession was a tremendous encouragement to this emerging movement: over 400 years ago, other Christians had believed and practised things that were central to their own community.

• David Nussbaum works for Oxfam as its finance director and is a member of a Baptist new church north-west of London. In a two-part article in Issues 2 and 3 (February & June 1993), he examined some of the vestiges of Christendom which indicate that rumours of its death might be premature. Arguing that many so-called "free churches" are accidentally non-established, he raised many questions about how Christians might deal with these vestiges in church and society.

• Tim Foley, one of the leaders of the Wood Green Mennonite Church, reflected in Issue 8 (February 1995) on the "Toronto Blessing" which was then impacting churches across Britain. One feature of the Anabaptist Network is the number of people involved who would identify to some degree with the charismatic movement and this issue of the journal explored the charismatic dimension of sixteenth-century Anabaptism and lessons which might be learned from this in assessing contemporary phenomena.

• Alun Morinan, who lectures in the Department of Life Sciences at the University of East London and is involved in "Conscience – the Peace Tax Campaign," insisted in an article on the topic of paying tax to support war in Issue 10 (October 1995) that "peacemaking is at the heart of Jesus' message and therefore Christian discipleship."

Subsequent issues have continued to explore the subject of peace and peacemaking.

• Anne Wilkinson-Hayes, then Social Action Advisor for the Baptist Union of Great Britain and now a pastor in Oxford, shared in an interview in Issue 12 (June 1996) her "dream" for local church life. "I long for my church to be an alternative community," she said, "I want it to be tangibly, robustly different from prevailing values." Deepened relationships, fun in friendships and environmental action were among several practical suggestions for moving towards such an alternative community.

• Lloyd Pietersen was responsible for the teaching programme of a large House Church in Bristol before commencing doctoral studies on the Pastoral Epistles. He has contributed two articles in Issues 17 and 18 (Spring & Summer 1998) which draw on his research and which address the question of the role of women in the church, grappling with the restrictions imposed in 1 Timothy but arguing that, for Anabaptists, these must be interpreted in the light of the way Jesus treated and empowered women. In an earlier article on the significance of the Pastorals for Anabaptists in Issue 15 (June 1997) he wrote, "one of the great strengths of the Anabaptist Network has been the desire to learn about the Anabaptist heritage and thus to develop a sense of historical perspective." He warned, however, that though there is much to learn from this heritage, "sixteenth-century Anabaptist solutions cannot be uncritically transposed into our late twentieth-century context." *Anabaptism Today* has attempted both to learn from history and to explore what discipleship in the radical tradition means today.

• Jane and Geoff Thorington-Hassell live in East London, where Jane is minister of a Baptist church; together they convene the East London study group. Interviewed in Issue 17 (Spring 1997), they both expressed indebtedness to Anabaptist insights, especially in relation to non-violence, community and questions of gender, but Geoff concluded, "I don't know whether we can call ourselves 'Anabaptists,' but we are certainly sympathetic to some of the tenets of Anabaptism and wanting to discover whether Anabaptist perspectives can be made relevant in an urban context." Jane and Geoff represent two other features of the network – many are involved in urban ministry, and some are drawn to aspects of the tradition without being fully persuaded of its adequacy.

• Andrew Francis is a United Reformed Church minister from Sevenoaks, who early in 1998 became the network's part-time development worker. In Issue 18 (Summer 1998) he reflected on experience with *Alpha*, a national evangelism programme which he had used in his church. Affirming much of this experience, he also raised questions from an Anabaptist perspective about the apparent emphasis on belief rather than discipleship and on individualism rather than community. Several issues of *Anabaptism Today* have included articles raising questions about evangelism, church planting and the mission of the church in a post-Christian society.

• Nelson Kraybill, now president of the Associated Mennonite Biblical Seminary in Elkhart, Indiana, was deeply involved in the development of the Anabaptist Network and was co-editor of *Anabaptism Today* during its early years. Two articles in Issues 10 and 11 (October 1995 and February 1996) on dealing creatively with conflict in the church were appreciated by many readers and reflected the commitment of the London Mennonite Centre to helping churches with this issue.

Anabaptists Today

These people, and others in the network, come from many traditions, drawn to Anabaptism for diverse reasons. Many members of the network seem to have little else in common except their interest in Anabaptism. Their paths would either never cross at all or, if they did, they might well be heading in opposite directions on many issues. Within the same network are Christians with very different views on ecclesiology, politics, mission, social involvement, spirituality and ethics. Conservatives and liberals, charismatics and contemplatives, Calvinists and Arminians, premillennialists and postmillennialists, are all finding in Anabaptism a shared heritage that transcends their different perspectives on other issues. What is it about the Anabaptist tradition that such a disparate group of people feel at home within it?

Some members of the network are historians or theologians, who have become intrigued by the sixteenth-century radicals. Some are exploring community living and look to the early Anabaptists for encouragement and guidance. Some are involved in peace organisations or justice ministries and draw strength from the Anabaptist tradition. Some are committed to urban mission and have discovered in

Anabaptism (in spite of its frequent association with rural culture) themes that help them to bring "good news to the poor." Many are committed to their denominations but are looking for ways to enrich them through contact with the Anabaptist tradition. Some are dissatisfied with their own experience of church and discipleship and are seeking a more satisfying alternative. A significant number of network members are church leaders, or those training to become church leaders.

The network has grown through relationships rather than through programmes or advertisements. Its roots are in a study group, convened by a Mennonite, Alan Kreider, and a Baptist, Nigel Wright, that met for several years in the 1980s at the London Mennonite Centre. Mennonites, Baptists and House Church leaders met together to explore a shared interest in things Anabaptist. We talked together, ate together, studied sixteenth-century documents, presented papers and became friends. The departure to Manchester in 1991 of Alan and Eleanor Kreider, who more than any others had introduced British Christians to the Anabaptist tradition, and the arrival of Nelson Kraybill as the new Programme Director at the London Mennonite Centre, coincided with a sense that we had stumbled on something that would be life-giving for many others. We wrote around to about eighty friends and contacts suggesting the formation of a network and the production of a journal and asking who else might be interested. We received a positive response and the network was born.

The significance of the network is not its size. The representatives of the Church of England who dialogued with us in October 1993 made it quite clear that they regarded this as a one-off event. The Anabaptist presence in the United Kingdom was too small to warrant further attention from the established church. Nor is the network significant because it has a manifesto for the future. We are such a diverse coalition that it is difficult to know what plans would receive widespread support. Some have suggested that in the current climate of church planting in the United Kingdom we should be planting new churches with an Anabaptist flavour; others would regard this as a counterproductive move and would rather see the network working for renewal within the existing structures. There are surely echoes here of the debates in the sixteenth century between those favouring reformation and those advocating a new beginning.

More significant perhaps than the numbers is that many church leaders are involved in the network. The influence of these men and women in local churches up and down the country could be profound as they draw on Anabaptist insights and work through the implications in their own ministries. This is vital if Anabaptist insights are to impact "ordinary" church members, rather than being restricted to esoteric discussions among ministers and historians. In partnership with Spurgeon's College, the network has developed an MTh course in Baptist and Anabaptist Studies, offering an opportunity to explore Anabaptism at a serious academic level. Given the history of Anabaptism in Britain and the limited awareness of Anabaptism in theological training circles, this course is an important resource. But the crucial challenge facing the network is to convey the essence of the Anabaptist tradition in ways that make sense to and empower local congregations and energise Christians attempting to be faithful disciples in their daily lives.

Anabaptist Churches?

Concern to work for the renewal of existing churches rather than developing a new denomination or institution has thus far discouraged the planting of Anabaptist churches, with the exception of the Wood Green Mennonite Church, which emerged from the London Mennonite Centre and is the only Mennonite church in the country.

But the question of whether we should develop Anabaptist churches has not gone away. Although we have no interest in denominational proliferation, close to the heart of Anabaptism is a vision of church life that enables people to follow Jesus together. Unless we have congregational expressions of the values that we embrace, how can the network promote these with integrity?

One response to this concern was a different kind of conference in January 1998, to which we invited groups of leaders from about twenty churches who were wanting to explore the relevance of Anabaptism for their own congregation. An exciting day together may lead to the development of another kind of network – a network of congregations rather than individuals. We have begun to offer Anabaptist resources to these congregations, to encourage cross-fertilisation and to plan further congregational conferences. We have toyed with the term "hyphenated-Anabaptist" to describe these congregations, which retain their denominational allegiance but acknowledge the value of Anabaptist perspectives and welcome links with other such churches.

Represented at the 1998 conference was an inner-city church planting initiative known as *Urban Expression*, whose co-ordinator Juliet Kilpin led our worship on that day. This initiative is planting new churches through the deployment of self-funding teams in some of the least churched areas of London. Although not overtly Anabaptist, many of the values and perspectives of this initiative are thoroughly compatible with the Anabaptist tradition and the churches which are planted may well be as Anabaptist as any in Britain. If church planting continues to be in vogue in Britain as the Decade of Evangelism draws to a close, then it may be that "Anabaptist churches," whatever they call themselves, will be among those planted over the next few years.

Anabaptist Perspectives

Harold Bender suggested in *The Anabaptist Vision*, his landmark paper on Anabaptism, that the Anabaptist vision included three major points of emphasis, namely: Christianity as discipleship, the church as brotherhood, and an ethic of love and non-resistance.[3] Many have challenged his choice of emphases, but his conclusions have proved to have enduring influence. Two of these emphases have already been recognised as significant by Christians in Britain who are becoming familiar with the Anabaptist tradition.

Discipleship and the church as a community (a preferable term to brotherhood) have been emphases that Christians from many traditions in Britain have been familiar with in recent years. There have been experiments with extended households and community of goods, especially in the 1970s as part of the charismatic renewal. The widespread use of home groups – and the more recent adoption of the cell church model – has weaned churches away from identifying the church as a building and introduced a deeper sense of family and community. A concern for making disciples rather than merely winning converts has been expressed in various ways – from trenchant criticisms of mass evangelism to shepherding movements and systems of church discipline that introduce new forms of accountability into church life. These emphases have not normally been derived from engagement with the

Anabaptist tradition, but they represent common ground that makes Anabaptist perspectives on these issues congenial across the ecclesiastical spectrum. The significance of the Anabaptist tradition on these issues is not that it introduces novel ideas but that it offers resources for renewal to those who have become wearied or disillusioned by their experiences of community or discipleship and need refreshment.

But the emphasis on non-resistance or, using a more positive term, peace has yet to be embraced by most churches in Britain. A surprising number of church members are committed privately to such a stance, but the official position in most churches and in all the main denominations is along the lines of the Just War theory. There has not been a strong "peace church" tradition in the United Kingdom, although the Quakers have kept this vision alive. The "peace movements" that briefly flourished in Britain and involved some church members are struggling in the post-Cold War era. Among members of the Anabaptist Network there would be no consensus on this issue. Some have urged us to refrain from giving the impression that Anabaptism implies pacifism and have pointed us to the diversity within sixteenth-century Anabaptism on this issue. Others are suggesting that "peace churches" should be planted or that denominations should be encouraged to identify with the peace church tradition. This is an issue on which Christians in Britain are far from united and have much still to learn from the discussions that have taken place within the Anabaptist tradition. Members of the network's steering group, however, are committed to peace and to exploring through *Anabaptism Today* biblical teaching on this theme and practical examples of peacemaking.

But there are other emphases in the Anabaptist tradition than those which Bender identified, some of which may be especially significant in the context of the British Isles. My own doctoral studies were in the area of Anabaptist hermeneutics[4] and I was profoundly impressed by many aspects of the way in which they handled the Bible. The enfranchisement of all believers as interpreters, the emphasis on application and obedience rather than intellectual understanding and the communal context for interpreting Scripture all seemed to me to have considerable contemporary significance – and some fascinating parallels with, for example, liberation theology. The lessons learned through the struggle to hold together Word and Spirit in sixteenth-century Anabaptism also offers resources to those who are concerned today to find ways to hold these vital elements together. But above all I was drawn to the Christocentric approach of most sixteenth-century Anabaptists. They took Jesus seriously and were not prepared to allow his teachings to be diluted. Jesus was for them the focal point of Scripture and the hermeneutical key that unlocked the meaning of both Testaments. I was left with concerns about the way many of them handled the Old Testament, but I was convinced that their Christocentrism had protected them from misinterpreting it in ways so many of their contemporaries were doing and so many interpreters have done since.

In many churches in Britain there is not a similar focus on Jesus Christ. The Epistles appear to be given prominence over the Gospels, the Old Testament is used as an adequate basis for ethical guidance and ecclesiological structure with no reference to the Christ-event, and much biblical interpretation is Christological (with Jesus functioning as a doctrinal centre) rather than Christocentric (where the teaching and example of Jesus is taken seriously). As a result, on various issues, from the practice of tithing to our attitude to violence, from the role of women in the church to our views on eschatology, Christians manage to be what I have come to call "biblically unchristian." Perhaps one area in which the Anabaptist Network can make a contribution is to challenge churches from various traditions to take Jesus much more seriously and to adopt a more Christocentric approach.

Another emphasis relates to my current role as the director of a church planting and evangelism course, training men and women to establish new congregations. Church planting has been high on the agenda of the British churches during the 1990s. Strategies have been developed to plant thousands of new churches all over the country. I am committed to church planting and am actively involved in a training and consultancy role, having worked for twelve years as a church planter in inner London. But I have some concerns about the way in which church planting is being perceived and pursued, and especially that little missiological or ecclesiological reflection is involved. Why should several thousand more churches of the kind we already have stem the flow of hundreds of church members from British churches each week?

I suspect that Anabaptist perspectives on missiology and ecclesiology might have a significant contribution to make. I already recommend to my students a book written by two Mennonites entitled *Creating Communities of the Kingdom*,[5] which reflects various Anabaptist insights on ecclesiology and mission. I have also been exploring through articles in *Anabaptism Today* some ways in which the sixteenth-century Anabaptist church planting movement in central Europe might be relevant to contemporary evangelistic and church planting practice.[6] The fact that these articles have already been reprinted in three other magazines suggests that the contribution of Anabaptism in this area is beginning to be valued. The contemporary church planting movement in the United Kingdom is unusually ecumenical (compared with most church planting in Europe over the past five centuries which has been sectarian), so in this area also the Anabaptist tradition has the potential to inform and challenge Christians from several traditions.

But if the Anabaptist vision has obvious potential within the British context, the Anabaptist Network faces some very real dangers. We have noted already the temptation to operate at an intellectual and theoretical level – something surely diametrically opposed to the nature of Anabaptism. There is also the danger of the Anabaptist vision being co-opted and domesticated by those who appreciate certain aspects of the tradition but fail to discern its true nature. Noel Moules, writing in *Anabaptism Today*, has warned: "In order to sound radical, the language of some groups and individuals is merely being decorated with 'Anabaptist-speak,' with no serious change to thinking or behaviour." Such "Anabaptist-speak" is becoming evident, as different groups claim an affinity with Anabaptism in order to appear radically respectable! It is difficult to know whether the Anabaptist vision is under greater threat from becoming respectable than from centuries of being marginalised.

Anabaptism in Britain, as noted above, is surprisingly ecumenical. A vision that in many other places has been perceived as sectarian and has been expressed in denominational forms has an opportunity to operate ecumenically in the United Kingdom and to challenge Christians in many denominations. Lacking a historical and ecclesiastical expression may be a weakness, in that there are few models to show what the vision means in practice. But the compensation for this is relative freedom from cultural accretions and an opportunity to explore issues of discipleship, mission and ecclesiology without inviting suspicions of denominational aggrandisement.

It may be that the growing interest in Anabaptism is but part of a much larger shift away from denominationalism towards a grass-roots ecumenism. Official ecumenical pronouncements, programmes and structures do not appear to excite much enthusiasm among most church members. Most attempts to plant ecumenical churches have failed miserably. But grass-roots ecumenism is flourishing. Denominational allegiance means less and less to church members under forty. Christians who move home look for other things than denominational labels as they search for a new church. The charismatic movement has played a significant role in this. The church planting movement is adding to what some might interpret as God-inspired confusion, in that church plants often have more in common with church plants in other denominations than with older churches from their own denomination.

We have a suspicion that Anabaptism is a timely addition to this ecclesiastical mix. The Anabaptist tradition remains remarkably potent and, for a perspective long regarded as sectarian, surprisingly ecumenical in its appeal. These are early days, we may be over-estimating the potential, we still need to grapple with the implications of the vision for ourselves. But we do sense that the Anabaptist vision can have a significant role to play in various churches in the United Kingdom in the coming years. For some, it will undergird their existing commitments; for others it will open up new possibilities and challenge them to more faithful and Christ-centred discipleship.

Anabaptism in Britain and North America

This book has two main audiences – British and North American. We want to encourage British Christians who are as yet unaware of the potency of the Anabaptist tradition to explore this marginalised expression of Christian discipleship. And we want to share with North American Christians, where the Anabaptist tradition is more familiar, the impact that this tradition is having in a nation with little or no Anabaptist history. Perhaps I can add here a comment or two that may be of special interest to our North American readers.

Those of us involved in exploring and promoting Anabaptist perspectives in Britain have greatly appreciated the interest, support and stimulation of many North American Mennonites, both in person and through your writings. They have had a greater influence in the United Kingdom than they perhaps realise – certainly much greater than the number of overtly Mennonite activities in Britain would suggest. We continue to need to draw on their scholarship, history and practical experience. American tourists are intrigued by the age of our towns and buildings and compare our long history with their much shorter history. But with regard to Anabaptism, they have by far the longer history and the practical experience of working out Anabaptist principles in a range of situations. We are just beginning and we have much to learn from them.

Can we offer anything in return? Perhaps I can suggest two possibilities. First, we might offer fresh insights from those who are exploring Anabaptism without centuries of inculturation. While we very much appreciate Mennonite understandings of Anabaptism, it may be that we who come from other traditions but share the conviction that the sixteenth-century Anabaptist vision has an enduring power will discover in this vision dimensions that have perhaps been overlooked or given only minimal attention. For example, as a charismatic researching into Anabaptism, I have become convinced that the sixteenth-century Anabaptists were much more charismatic than is usually acknowledged by historians. Their hermeneutics, ecclesiology, missiology and spirituality were all affected by this dimension. Of course, I am as much in danger of reading back my prejudices into the sixteenth century as Mennonites have sometimes been accused of doing, but at least I bring some different prejudices with me! A large number of those attracted to Anabaptism in Britain are charismatics, often without being aware of any charismatic dimension within Anabaptism. As they discover this dimension and reflect on their own experience, I suspect that not only will their interest in Anabaptism grow but that new expressions of charismatic Anabaptism will develop.

Second, Britain is moving rapidly into a thoroughly post-Christendom culture and in this is some years ahead of North America, although a similar trend is evident there. We live in a society where churchgoing is increasingly counter-cultural and where the political and social influence of the church is now marginal. In such a society many perspectives and values inherited from the dominant Catholic and Protestant traditions – which fought each other but both continued to operate under the Christendom system – seem less helpful now that Christendom is fading.

By contrast, some aspects of the Anabaptist tradition – which centuries ago identified Christendom as essentially inimical to faith and discipleship – seem surprisingly relevant. Many Christians are finding insights and resources from this tradition within which the values and reflexes of Christendom have received a trenchant and sustained critique. It may be that North American Mennonites will find helpful some of the lessons we are learning, in conversation with Anabaptism, as we explore what it means to follow Jesus "after Christendom" rather than yearning nostalgically for the restoration of a largely mythical "Christian nation."

Third, the emergence of an Anabaptist network in Britain may offer North American Anabaptists an opportunity to observe the impact of the Anabaptist vision in an ecumenical context, where there are no Anabaptist denominations in operation, and where Anabaptist perspectives are interacting with different traditions than those it interacts with in North America. It may be that watching and interacting with these developments will stimulate new insights and perceptions for them also. Anabaptism in the United Kingdom could almost be regarded as a laboratory experiment. How will the Anabaptist vision that has so often been perceived as sectarian impact a nation without significant Anabaptist influences in its history? What is the ecumenical potential of this vision?

Anabaptism Elsewhere?

Shortly before submitting the final draft of this essay, I had a conversation with a Christian leader from Korea who was visiting Britain and staying at the London Mennonite Centre. He was interested in learning about the development of the Anabaptist Network here and eager to hear of similar developments in other nations. He was in the process of setting up an Anabaptist Centre in Korea. He was also exploring the feasibility of arranging an international conference for representatives of Anabaptist networks and resource centres in many nations.

As we shared information about our contacts with such people in various nations, it began to dawn on me that our experience in the British Isles might not be unique. In other nations with as limited an Anabaptist heritage as ours, the Anabaptist tradition was also being discovered, networks were emerging, and many other people were "coming home" to a way of following Jesus that makes sense in a post-Christendom world.

Networks have been identified as key features of a postmodern society, alternatives to the large institutions that dominated modernity. Unlike such institutions, grass-roots networks do not require impressive buildings, large amounts of finance or bulky support structures. What do such networks need if they are to develop? What can the experience of the Anabaptist Network in the British Isles offer to those involved in emerging networks elsewhere?

- networks depend on friendships and multiple personal links;
- networks need enough events or activities to maintain momentum but not so many as to wear out participants;
- networks require strategists with the ability to envision, organise and facilitate;
- networks take time to develop and those involved will need to be patient;
- networks need to develop various ways of communicating information, vision and values;
- networks can allow people to participate in various ways and at various levels;
- networks need not be exclusive or threatening to other networks or institutions, as participants can belong to several networks.

We offer the stories and essays in this book as a resource for others. We look forward to hearing stories from developing Anabaptist networks in other nations and even to the formation of a global network in the coming years.

NOTES

[1] See Ian Randall's article, "Early English Baptists and Religious Liberty," *Anabaptism Today* (October 1993):10-16.

[2] See Ian Randall's article cited above.

[3] Harold Bender, *The Anabaptist Vision* (Scottdale: Herald Press,1944):20.

[4] Stuart Murray, "Spirit, Discipleship, Community: The Contemporary Significance of Anabaptist Hermeneutics" (unpublished thesis, The Open University, 1994), now published as *Biblical Interpretation in the Anabaptist Tradition* (Kitchener, ON: Pandora Press, 2000).

[5] David Shenk and Ervin Stutzman, *Creating Communities of the Kingdom* (Scottdale:Herald Press,1988).

[6] Stuart Murray, "A Decade of Evangelism," *Anabaptism Today* (February 1993):3-7 and "Evangelism in the Radical Tradition," *Anabaptism Today* (October 1993):4-9.

When Anabaptists were last in the British Isles

Alan Kreider

It was Easter morning, April 3, 1575. About two dozen people – fifteen women, ten men and a young lad – were gathered in "a suburb" near Aldgate, which was then on the edge of London. They were foreigners, refugees from Flanders, who had come together "to hear the Word of God" and to pray. At nine o'clock, there was a knock at the door.[1] Tipped off by the neighbours that something suspicious was afoot, a constable entered, accompanied by several beadles. The constable was rough with the refugees. He "called them devils," wrote down their names, and then arrested them. In the ensuing three months, these obscure aliens became a preoccupation of the most notable figures in England.[2]

Several days after Easter, the prisoners had visitors. An impressive group, comprising Edwin Sandys, Bishop of London, two aldermen, three English preachers and one French preacher, came to confront them with four articles, which they must sign or be burnt alive. This was not a time for nuances: they must "say yes or no."

1. That Christ had assumed his flesh and blood from the substance of the flesh and blood of Mary.
2. That infants ought to be baptised.
3. That a Christian might administer the office of a magistrate.
4. That a Christian might swear an oath.

When the Anabaptist refugees replied cautiously – that they could not find *this* in the Scriptures, or that their consciences would not allow *that* – the bishop replied, according to one of the Anabaptists who survived, "that our crimes were very great, so that we should not inherit the Kingdom of God."

Back in the Mersey prison, the Anabaptists continued their attempt to explain their position. They wrote a general letter giving a reasoned defence of their positions and of their social vision – "what we seek and desire here upon earth." Three weeks of solitary confinement, "with fetters on our legs," assisted them in reflecting on their errors. Now and then their isolation was punctuated by visits, both by members of the Dutch Church in London and by an emissary of the bishop; the latter said that the bishop had promised that "if we would adhere to the church, he would release us, and free us from our bonds." Five of the prisoners, all men, gave in to pressure. On 25 June, at Paul's Cross outside St. Paul's Cathedral in the heart of London, in the presence of "many thousand Englishmen" and directly in front of the pulpit, these five carried faggots symbolic of their deserving of death. Mercifully, Bishop Sandys announced that they, who had been "seduced," would now be joining the Dutch [Reformed] Church and thus "become [our] brethren."

On 11 May, five weeks after their arrest, a Commission under the Great Seal was appointed to examine, hear and determine concerning the Anabaptists. It was an august body, made up of the Bishops of London and Rochester, two deans, the Master of Rolls and two justices of the Common Pleas.[3] Ten days later, the prisoners were called in, two by two, before the Commissioners, who urged them to sign the four questions. When the prisoners refused, they were divided: the fourteen women and a young lad were "tied hand to hand" and sent to Newgate, "which is the prison of those confined for capital crimes." The women thought that they would be the first to be burnt. Day by day officials came to visit them, "holding up death before their eyes, if they should not renounce." Other visitors came, some to convert them. William White, a baker, brought the women a book of a Mr. Calvin to have them "read his words"; they refused, saying they "did not depend on men."[4] Another visitor, an anonymous man with the initials of "S.B.," came to inquire of the prisoners: "my chief desire," he later confessed, "is to be among the children of God and such as follow the life of Christ most near, and I so esteem of them that I think them worthy of reverence, yea thinking myself if I may be but a hewer of wood and drawer of water among them."[5] But S.B. was exceptional, and after all was only a carpenter. And soon the women, from whom he thought he could learn so much, were carted to a ship at St Catherine's Dock and deported to Holland. Tied to the front of the cart and whipped as he went along was the young lad, who blurted out, "This is for the name of Christ."

Meanwhile, attempts were being made to forestall the execution of the rest of the prisoners. In this, members of the Dutch Church were notably active. So also were members of the French Church, who petitioned the Council, emphasising "the simplicity of these people."[6] Perhaps the most impassioned intervention came in a letter to Queen Elizabeth from the martyrologist John Foxe.[7] These appeals notwithstanding, the process against the heretics continued. On 2 June, Bishop Sandys called the five prisoners before his episcopal court at St Paul's. Once again he confronted them with the four articles, in default of which they were to be burned at Smithfield. One of the prisoners, Jan Pieterss, replied that this "was a small matter." This outraged Sandys, who proceeded to "expel them from his church, as bad members." Whereupon a second prisoner, Hendrick Terwoort, spoke up. "How can you expel us from your church, when we have never yet been one with you?" Sandys replied: "That this was all the same, . . . [for] in England there was no one that was not a member of God's church." He then "condemned them all to death" and handed them over to the secular arm.

The five male prisoners were now transferred to the Newgate prison, from which the women had recently been deported. The prison authorities confined the Anabaptists among thieves and criminals, "to whom the bishop . . . said that they should take care not to be seduced by us." Their imprisonment was severe, in a "deep dungeon" where they, according to one prisoner, "were confined in cages, so that we could not converse with our neighbours." Death was "from day to day announced to us, by hanging, burning and otherwise." In this situation of *extremis* the prisoners somehow engaged in more writing. To John Foxe – who although advocating their cause had written to them "somewhat severely" about their obstinacy and theological perversity, "which overthrow our salvation" – the prisoners wrote stating some of their central convictions. They also wrote to the Queen. In this they were wasting their time. When some maids of honour attempted to present a letter in which the Anabaptists made an appeal to her, she reprimanded the women – and refused to touch the tainted paper.

The Queen then set the legal processes in motion for ending the crisis: she ordered Lord Chancellor Bacon to prepare a writ *de haeretico comburendo*, "for the execution of justice . . . and to give example to others lest they should attempt the like hereafter."[8] On 5 July, Bacon issued the writ,[9] but it was not put into effect for almost three weeks. These were days of hectic activity. The government, working through Bishop Sandys, used the time to issue articles to which *all foreigners* in London, and not simply the prisoners in Newgate, must subscribe. Meanwhile, in prison, one of the five prisoners died "through . . . hardship of the severe confinement." The four remaining Anabaptists attempted to contact friends outside. They also were visited by ministers, who in various ways did their best to get them to save their lives by recanting. One minister, for example, "laying his hands upon them, and falling down upon his knees, cried aloud: 'Lord, convert their heart'; and naming the devil, said, 'Depart from them, thou wicked one.'" On 17 July, it was announced that "the oldest two" – Pieterss and Terwoort – should be executed.

Five days later, in front of a varied audience of dignitaries and common people, Jan Pieterss and Hendrick Terwoort were burned at Smithfield. On his way to the stake, Terwoort asserted to the crowds: "This way went all the pious prophets, as also Christ our Saviour." At the stake, the prisoners were given a final opportunity to assent to the four articles. They refused and were executed in the slowest way possible, "without any strangling or gunpowder." Anabaptist accounts emphasise the fortitude of the martyrs; an English chronicler, on the other hand, reports that the prisoners died as heretics are supposed to die, "in great horror with roaring and crying."[10] At the time of his death Terwoort, a goldsmith, had been married for less than half a year; he was 35. The other victim, Jan Pieterss, was a "poor man" of unknown occupation aged 50. His first wife had been burned in Ghent; together he and she left nine children to the care of his second wife, "whose [first] husband had also previously been burned in Ghent for his religion."

With the burnings of Pieterss and Terwoort there were now only two prisoners left to languish in Newgate. These eventually, despite an attempt to escape by "filing off an iron bar," were released the following year.[11] Elizabeth and her Councillors evidently felt that the two executions had made their point.

How do we know about these events? We know about them in part because the Anabaptists left letters and accounts. For example, one of the surviving men, Gerrit van Byler, while still a prisoner had written a narrative to encourage Anabaptists on the continent who were also being persecuted. Other Anabaptists saved copies of the prisoners' letters to the Queen and to John Foxe. A vital source is a long letter by the Flemish Calvinist Jacques de Somere, who helped the Anabaptists draft their statements. All of these writings were passed down among Dutch Mennonites. And, in 1660, this entire corpus of materials was collected by the Dordrecht Mennonite preacher Thielemann J. van Braght who included them, with his own introduction, in his massive martyrology, *The Martyrs Mirror*, an Anabaptist counterpart to Foxe's *Acts and Monuments*. English chronicles, correspondence and governmental sources provide additional detail and corroborate the main outlines of the Anabaptists' records. My account is a reconstruction drawing from all of these sources.

Why tell the story? The topic that was assigned to me for the occasion when this paper was first given was "Mennonite/Anabaptist Perceptions of Relationships with the Church of England – the Sixteenth Century." And since there are very few encounters between Anglicans and those who were clearly Anabaptists in the continental tradition, this account, which according to a contemporary source[12] clearly involves "Menno's people," is of particular value. Nor are there many other accounts of English people who had espoused Anabaptist ideas. Joan Bocher and Robert Cooche held views that coincided with those of many Anabaptists, but they were not part of Anabaptist congregations.[13] To be sure, there were many people who called others, whom they for some reason didn't like, Anabaptists. "Anabaptist" was the way that one stigmatised someone whose social or theological stance was more radical than one's own. But everyone in the period agreed: there were no English Anabaptist congregations, and there were very few English Anabaptists. John Foxe, who should have known, wrote to the Queen that "today I see none of the English touched by this madness."[14] Protestant publicist and Edwardian Bishop John Bale agreed: "I never heard it, that ever any man within the realm, went about the reiteration of baptism."[15]

From prison the persecuted Flemings substantially concurred: "They pretend that there are so many thousands of us in the country, who want to take possession of countries and cities; whereas no such thoughts have entered into our hearts, for it is impossible to take possession of countries and cities without violence and bloodshed . . .

We have not so easy a faith, that they flock to us in crowds; only here and there may be a household, which are very solitary." Were the Anabaptists referring to "S.B." who visited the women in prison?[16] Or to another English Anabaptist whom we know about, John Bret, who was burned for heresy in Ghent in the following year?[17] We don't know. What is quite clear to scholars today is that "it cannot be positively proved that any 'gathered' congregation, rejecting the whole concept of a state church, existed in England at any time between 1530 and 1570."[18] Nor can it be shown that there were English Christians who, during this period, actually practised believers' baptism. The term English Anabaptism, during this period, is a contradiction in terms.

Nevertheless, there was a fear of Anabaptism, which is expressed in the strongest of terms and at times appears almost desperate, among English Protestants. This appears from the earliest times of the English Reformation. In my own Reformation researches I discovered in the Public Record Office an anonymous draft, which did not quite make it into the Ten Articles of 1536, which asserted the necessity of continuing the long-established practice of baptising infants. "And all the Anabaptists' opinions contrary to it . . . to be reputed among us [to be] heresies erroneous & detestable."[19] Charles Hardwick's researches into the 42 Articles of 1553 indicated that no fewer than half were in one way or another directed against the Anabaptists.[20] Of these, fifteen were incorporated in the Elizabethan 39 Articles, which remain part of the Christian inheritance which defines Anglican identity, including Article 38:

The riches and goods of Christians are not common, as touching the right, title, and possession of the same, as certain Anabaptists do falsely boast.

Everyone wanted to disassociate themselves from these people. Radical Puritans such as John Field were especially eager to make clear that *they* weren't "subverters of all good order . . . proud, arrogant, ambitious, troublers of common weals, Anabaptists, and such like."[21] Many common people shared these prejudices. It is striking that the Anabaptist house church near the Aldgate was reported to the authorities by their neighbours, who may have combined, in a fashion that has not altogether disappeared, a certain

Why were these people so fearful? There were no doubt many reasons. But at the root of their fears was a deep-seated concern for social cohesion. In England, as throughout much of Europe, rulers and churchmen were aware of the eighteen-month "Kingdom of Saints" in Münster, in which so-called Anabaptists by political and then by military means instituted a theocracy on Old Testament lines. With great loss of life it was besieged into submission by the prince bishop. To sixteenth-century people Münster became a byword for revolutionary mayhem. All parts of the Anabaptist movement, led in northern Europe by the ex-priest Menno Simons, repudiated the ethics and the social strategy of Münster. And, from prison, our prisoners likewise disavowed "the Münsterite errors or abominations." But Münster continued to function as a symbol of what even the pacifist Anabaptists represented, a phenomenon, in the words of the anti-Anabaptist proclamation which Elizabeth I issued at the start of her reign, of "fanatical and heretical opinions."[22] That is, of something enshrining erroneous Christian teaching which led to the subversion of ordered social life.

Ordered social life was, to be sure, under threat in the mid-sixteenth century. The assumptions and institutions of Christendom, which had been largely unquestioned for a millennium, were now beginning to disintegrate. The English people, as Tudor succeeded Tudor, were being assaulted by competing views of the truth. The unity of the Christian world was being shattered by the emergence of national churches. Peasants, with centuries of grievance behind them, were taking advantage of the uncertainties of the times to query traditional loyalties. In 1575, moderate Protestantism seemed to be in the ascendancy in England, but many, of both Roman Catholic and radical Protestant persuasion, were dissatisfied and biding their time. In this setting of uncertainty, many people felt it to be of paramount importance to maintain the underlying assumptions of Christendom, which seemed to transcend all party division. And it was precisely these assumptions, dating from the fourth and fifth centuries, that the very existence of the Anabaptists seemed to threaten. We today can see the Anabaptists in other ways: as pioneers of a new world, a post-Christendom world; or as embodiments of a "subversive memory" of an earlier, pre-Christendom world. But to Bishop Sandys and his colleagues the Anabaptists appeared to be wreckers: "What stirs diversity of religion hath raised in nations and kingdoms . . . Division weakeneth; concord strengtheneth."[23] Similarly, the Puritan John Field derided the Anabaptists for societal fragmentation and "many hurlyburlys."[24]

But what were the Anabaptists' views? In what ways did they conceive of themselves as pioneering a new world? It is impossible neatly to generalise, for the Anabaptist movement was decentralised; spread all over Europe it encompassed many traditions. But we can get an initial sense of the Anabaptists' challenge by listening to these prisoners and attempting to express their perceptions of the Church of England. In doing so, I must concede that their perceptions were at times ill-informed: the Flemish Anabaptists since their arrival in England seem largely to have kept to themselves (and for good reason, we might think), so at times they read the English situation through their experience of the Roman Catholics in Flanders. Their perceptions were also at times, in my view, arrogantly uncharitable: what right did they have to assert that the Anglican clergy, across the board, were "not fit persons to administer such an office?"[25] And yet there are, I believe, other points at which the Anabaptist perceptions of the Church of England are worth listening to. Let me mention six.

Perception 1: Heresy. The Anabaptists knew that the Church of England's leaders called them "heretics." Such language was characteristic of a Christianity which since the fourth century had placed primary importance upon faith as the correct formulation of words, ideas, and propositions. After three centuries in which Christian leaders had devoted themselves to forming communities of distinctive lifestyle, in which truth was as much *lived* truth as truth to be articulated, in the fourth century the church gave its most creative efforts to "creeds, councils and controversies."[26] By the end of the fourth century, the creators of Christendom – theologians and emperors working together – were stigmatising those whose theological formulations were adjudged erroneous as "demented and insane," whose "meeting places shall not receive the name of churches, and they shall be smitten first by divine vengeance and secondly by the retribution" of the imperial power.[27]

The Anabaptists were not, however, convinced by all aspects of post-fourth-century theologising. It was not that they always got things right. The doctrine which the first of the four articles denounced is, in my opinion, one example of this. The "celestial flesh" of Christ, in which Christ took his human flesh not "from" Mary but "out of" Mary, was an Anabaptist distinctive. Although it is likely that this teaching was derived from non-Anabaptist sources (especially Caspar Schwenckfeld, Sebastian Franck and Clement Ziegler), it was adopted and adapted by Dutch Anabaptists. Hoffman enunciated it in 1529, citing John 6:33, which refers to Jesus as the bread which comes down from heaven to give life to the world; Menno Simons like the prisoners in Newgate never preached it, but under attack they defended it. The doctrine's main concern seems to have been to express strongly the novelty of God's action in the New Adam. With Christ something entirely new has entered the world; and he, by grace, has ushered into being a new creation which takes on social expression, e.g. in a community that lives the disarmed life. The Dutch Anabaptists, our prisoners included, were vehement that this doctrine of the incarnation was congruent with an acceptance of the full humanity of Christ. Whether they got this right may or may not be worth discussing; most sixteenth-century Anabaptists never held the doctrine of Christ's celestial flesh, and the Anabaptists of Northern Europe have long since abandoned it.

But what is noteworthy is this: the church authorities viewed an amateurly construed statement on the incarnation as heresy to be extirpated at all costs, but they did not consider their own behaviour to be a deviation from the gospel or the earliest Christian traditions. To the Anabaptists, truth was not only a matter of correct verbal formulation; it was also a matter of one's life stance and one's discipleship. To them it was a matter of truth, indeed of orthodoxy, to "walk as Christ walked." A faith that was true enabled people not only to hear what the Christians say but to "see what we believe" in acts of costly obedience to Jesus Christ. A central illustration of their argument was the phenomenon of persecution. This characteristic practice of the ancient pagans, which had scandalised the Christians of the early centuries, now in its Christendom form in comparable fashion outraged the Anabaptists. How is it, they queried, that persecution is not wrong teaching? Why isn't persecution heresy? As our prisoners put it, "Those who hold the true evangelical doctrine and faith [i.e., who are orthodox] will persecute no one, but will themselves be persecuted." If they were, according even to gentle John Foxe, a people marked by "madness," this seems to me to have been a moment of fleeting lucidity!

Perception 2: Establishment. The Anabaptists viewed the Church of England as being in an alliance, incomprehensible to them, with the Civil Power. Of course the Christians of the early centuries could not have assumed such an alliance, and major readjustments were made in the fourth and following centuries when emperors presented themselves to the Church as Christians. But, although throughout the Christendom centuries the shape of this alliance needed recurrently to be negotiated, it was assumed that, as the Theodosian Code put it, "heresy is to be construed to be an offence against the state."[28] It was also assumed that monarchs, regardless of whether they "walked as Christ walked," were Christians. It would therefore be their responsibility, as the "secular arm," to carry out the capital punishment of heretics, "seeing that the *spiritual* justice ought never to put anyone to death."[29] Bishop Sandys put it neatly in one of his sermons: "One God, one king, one faith, one profession, is fit for one monarchy and commonwealth."[30]

The Anabaptists found this an unacceptable system. Christianity, they never tired of saying, was not a matter of labels; it was a matter of relationships and allegiances. It meant saying "yes" to Jesus as Lord, and by that allegiance to evaluate all other allegiances. The Anabaptists met, in their Church of England interlocutors, people who did not seem to see the possibility of this conflict of allegiances, at least not in Protestant England. For example, the Anabaptists encountered a Commission under the Great Seal containing members both ecclesiastical and civil, both deans of great churches and justices of the common pleas. And they encountered, in Queen Elizabeth, a ruler who attempted to set the rules in church as well as state. Was *she* a Christian? The Anabaptists, of course, to use one of Elizabeth's own expressions, could "not make windows into a woman's soul." But if they thus could not know whether she *knew* Jesus, they could hazard an opinion as to whether she was obeying him. And they encountered Elizabeth, as they had encountered other monarchs in Flanders, as the embodiment of policies that seemed to disobey Jesus, policies of violence and persecution.

Our Anabaptists were willing to agree, on grounds of Romans 13, that rulers were the servants of God. Under immense pressure in prison they were also ready to concede that just as the rich person, by God's infinite capacity to do the impossible, can be saved, so also a ruler can be a Christian, though "to human eyes it will, for manifold obstacles, be difficult"[31] – the manifold obstacles being the obvious reality in early modern Europe that governments did precious little for the people other than wield the sword. But the Anabaptists believed that Christ in the Sermon on the Mount called monarchs, along with all Christians, to engage in two practices which the third and fourth of their articles required them to renounce: to love the enemy and thus not to wield weapons; and to tell the truth and thus not to swear oaths. Of course, for the Anabaptists to refuse to fight and to swear had social consequences – these refusals posed uncomfortable but not unanswerable questions about national security and the operation of the courts. But a church newly established by act of Parliament in a situation of perceived peril could not begin to address those questions. Clinging to the Christendom tradition, it resorted to persecution.

Perception 3: Ecclesiology. The Anabaptists viewed the Church of England as a church which was based upon compulsion and which therefore, although it claimed to be equivalent with the entire population of England, could not be that. In their exchange with Bishop Sandys they heard the received position: "That in England there was no one that was not a member of God's church."[32] Everyone was a member of the church – the church as territorially conceived. But the Anabaptists pointed out that *they*, though residents of England, were not members of this church; and they argued that many others, who might view themselves as members of the church, were behaving in ways (fornicating, extorting, coveting) that Paul had said are incompatible with church membership (1 Corinthians 5.7-11). Indeed, it was clear to them, as to all observers of mid-sixteenth century life, that vast numbers of people didn't behave like Jesus taught and didn't even go to church. For that reason, explained Bishop Sandys, there had to be compulsion. "To see the gospel everywhere preached, the ministers provided for, and the people compelled to come to hear the word" – these are the responsibilities of the civil power.[33]

The Anabaptists, on the other hand, in the tradition of early Christianity which Augustine of Hippo repudiated, did not believe that anybody, certainly not the state, could compel faith. "It is impossible," they asserted, "to believe differently from what we feel in our conscience."[34] Compulsion, they were convinced, simply doesn't work. It doesn't produce a membership of committed disciples who will live the life of Jesus on the earth. Furthermore, it won't last: when compulsion disappears, the people will disappear. A true church, the Anabaptists were convinced, would instead be made up of people who would be volunteers. It would be an intentional church, a church of people who had been inwardly renewed and thus who outwardly would commit their lives to walking as Christ walked and to being "one with each other." Within every territory, indeed within the area claimed by every national church, they would live the life of resident aliens. As their understanding developed under pressure, the prisoners manifested what one might term an incipient Christian pluralism: they recognised that other Christians, in this case members of the Church of England, would hold different views on baptism, and they stated, "We do not condemn the churches that hold other views."[35]

Perception 4: Baptism. The Anabaptists disagreed with the baptismal understandings and practices of the Church of England, and of the other churches in the Christendom tradition. They perceived these as being yet another expression of religious compulsion. Baptism was important to the Anabaptists, and not only because it had come to be a part of their name. Through baptism our prisoners had freely entered into a new world, a world of life and of death, of intentional family and of risk of persecution. Through their baptism they had died to Christendom. They viewed this as a matter of obedience to biblical teaching. In one of their apologetic letters our prisoners argued against infant baptism at some length. They attempted to deal with arguments advanced by their antagonists, with original sin, circumcision and the rest. They denied, on rather unlearned historical grounds (although the best in contemporary patristic scholarship is surprisingly sympathetic to their view[36]), that infant baptism was the practice of the early Christians. They attempted instead to establish the importance in true baptism of reason and understanding, of faith and personal commitment. But their deepest reason, it seems to me, comes in an aside. "They accuse us of being disobedient to the magistracy, because we do not have our children baptised." Baptism into Christ's death and into Christ's life could not, they were convinced, be a matter of compulsion, either for parents or for their "speechless children." These views, to the authorities trying to keep Christendom intact, were inflammatory, hence the second of the four articles condemning the Anabaptists.

Perception 5: Hermeneutics. The Anabaptists sensed that the spokesmen of the Church of England had an inconsistent method of biblical interpretation, and they said so. Bishop Sandys and other English clergy justified their persecution of the Anabaptists by Deuteronomy 13:5: "It is the Lord's commandment, 'Let the false prophet die.'"[37] If that be the case, the Anabaptists reasoned, the churchmen should also give expression to other prescriptions in Deuteronomy: "we should have to kill not only the false prophets, but also the adulterers, whoremongers, and those who take the name of the Lord in vain and curse."[38] In the New Testament, as well, the Anabaptists – like all those on the deviant fringe of Christendom – repeatedly encountered that blunderbuss of proof texts, Romans 13:1. The Anabaptists acknowledged this text, but maintained that it must be read in the wider context of New Testament teaching. Ultimately, our prisoners seem to have had an intuitive hermeneutic, whereby the words and way of Jesus provided an interpretive key to the rest of the Scriptures. For the advocates of Christendom, on the other hand, the interpretive key seems to have been stability. They had a hermeneutic of the status quo, the correct interpretation being one which does not rock the boat.

Perception 6: Learning and Status. The Anabaptists, who viewed themselves as simple folk, viewed the representatives of the Church of England as their cultural and intellectual superiors. In this they were correct. But it is also fascinating to see the humble but genuine self-respect of the Anabaptists. They had not been to university, but they had minds and consciences, and the capacity for independent thought. "Base things, and things which are most despised, hath God chosen, and things which are not, to them it is given to know the mysteries of the kingdom of God."[39] It is fascinating to see the Anabaptists hold on to this self-respect even as the weight of the Establishment (well-dressed churchmen and officers of the law) was brought to bear upon their dishevelled bodies crawling with vermin. They were told that they should submit to the superior learning of the ministers, to recognise the experience and authority of the great men and woman of the realm. To some extent we can see the prisoners begin to crack. Their language became even humbler. Writing to the Queen, they wrote, "We are a poor, simple people, of humble knowledge and understanding, and we are sorry that we cannot write more courteously."[40]

Yet with the exception of the five men who recanted early, the fourteen women, the young lad, and the five men didn't crack. "It is indeed possible," they wrote to John Foxe, "that through fear of death we could be made to *speak* differently from what we understand; but that we should *understand* otherwise than we believe, you know to be impossible."[41] They were holding on, it seems to me, to the intuition that they could see things which others were missing. The gospel talks about persecution, but never about imposing it; persecution, as numerous New Testament texts pointed out which the Anabaptists never tired of quoting, is the price of following Jesus seriously. Thus the Anabaptists could, perhaps with a wry smile, appropriate to themselves the Pauline self-designation – "the off-scouring of all things" (1 Corinthians 4:13). And we might, as we contemplate their day and ours, begin to ask, "In what social setting can one best read the Bible with understanding? Is there perhaps a hermeneutical privilege of the 'off-scoured?'"

What, then, is the significance of this story from sixteenth-century England? We include it here not because it represents the origins of Anabaptism in England – that story is a complex one, and extends over a century and more.[42] Nor is this story one which represents the views that all Anabaptist-inclined people in England would have in this period – the Anabaptists have always been diverse. Rather, we include this story because it is a potent story which does shed light on the deepest concerns of the Anabaptists and of the conservators of Christendom religion in England. Furthermore, this event represents a decisive silencing of Anabaptism, a gagging of the Anabaptist voice, which has, in our view, made the recent recovery of that voice which the current volume describes all the more necessary.[43]

For the next three and a half centuries there was no Anabaptist presence in the British Isles; the Anabaptist voice had been effectively silenced. Those in the British Isles who have found themselves drawn to the Anabaptist tradition in recent years cannot find an indigenous heritage within which to find a "home." But the perceptions of the Anabaptist prisoners have a remarkably contemporary feel, for the Christendom which was beginning to fall apart in the 1570s is now in disintegration. Some of their convictions are now widely accepted; others remain contentious. The insights of the spiritual descendants of both the Anabaptist prisoners and their Anglican interlocutors will both be necessary to face the challenges of the emerging post-Christendom environment. But it is important that the Anabaptist voice is no longer silenced but is heard among many others.

To be witnesses to Jesus Christ in our time and servants of the world that is no longer "Christian" but that he loves so much, both traditions are needed, bringing our riches, bringing our repentant learnings, bringing our capacity to imagine new things. We both have much to learn, not least from the early church from whose special qualities both of our traditions have sought direction. Above all, I suspect, we will be of most use to God's purposes in our time if we meet in the common affirmation of a text at the beginning of the story of Jesus in the Gospel of Luke that the Church of England sings in every Evensong: "His mercy is on them that fear him, through all generations. He hath shewed strength with his arm; he hath scattered the proud in the imagination of their hearts. He hath put down the mighty from their seat; and hath exalted the humble and meek." These words, quintessentially Anglican yet congenial to the Anabaptists, express the work of God in Jesus which is ever new, ever appropriate, and always challenging.

NOTES

[1] Edmond Howes, *Chronicle*, in John Strype, *Annales* (London, 1631):679.

[2] Thieleman Jansz van Braght, *Het Bloedig Toneel of Martelaers Spiegel der Doops-Gesinde of Weerelose Christenen* (Amsterdam: Hieronymus Sweerts, et al., 1685), II:694-712; translated by Joseph F. Sohm: *The Bloody Theater or Martyrs Mirror of the Defenceless Christians who Baptized Only upon Confession of Faith* (Scottdale,

PA: Herald Press, 1951)(henceforth *MM*).The following account is based largely upon the documents in this collection; full citations would in my estimation overload the scholarly apparatus. I do, however, provide citations for other sources used.

[3] Thomas Rymer, *Foedera* (London, 1713):15, 741.

[4] "Mr White's Writings," in Albert Peel: "A Conscientious Objector of 1575," *Transactions of the Baptist Historical Society*, 7 (1920-1921):78.

[5] *Ibid.*, 112.

[6] Patrick Collinson, *Godly People: Essays on English Protestantism and Puritanism* (London: The Hambledon Press, 1983):267n-268n.

[7] John Foxe to Elizabeth I, n.d. (late May 1575), in Thomas Fuller (ed.), *The Church History of Britain from the Birth of Jesus Christ until the Year MDCXLVIII* (London: William Tegg, 1868), II:576-577.

[8] Rymer, *Foedera*, 15: 740-741.

[9] *Ibid.*, 741

[10] Howes, *Chronicle*, in Strype, *Annales*, 679.

[11] "Mr White's Writings," in Peel, "A Conscientious Objector," 119-120.

[12] *MM*, 1047.

[13] On these, see M.T. Pearse, *Between Known Men and Visible Saints: A Study in Sixteenth-Century English Dissent* (Cranbury, N.J.: Associated University Presses, 1994); *idem*, "Robert Cooche and Anabaptist Ideas in Sixteenth-Century England," *Mennonite Quarterly Review*, 67 (1993):337-350.

[14] Foxe to Queen Elizabeth, n.d. (late May 1575), in Fuller, *Church History*, II:576.

[15] John Bale, *A Declaration of Edmonde Bonners articles* (London, 1561), Si[r], cited by Meic Pearse, "Fear of 'Anabaptists' in Sixteenth-Century England," *Anabaptism Today*, 3 (June 1993):22.

[16] Peel, "A Conscientious Objector," 74-75.

[17] *MM*, 1037.

[18] David Loades, "Anabaptism and English Sectarianism in the Mid-Sixteenth Century," in Derek Baker (ed.), *Reform and Reformation: England and the Continent, c1500 – c 1750*, Studies in Church History, Subsidia, 2 (Oxford: Basil Blackwell, 1979):70.

[19] P.R.O. SP 6/1, fo 2; for comment, see Alan Kreider, "An English Episcopal Draft Article Against the Anabaptists, 1536," *Mennonite Quarterly Review*, 49 (1975):48-52.

[20] Charles Hardwick, *A History of the Articles of Religion* (Cambridge: John Deighton, 1859):98-106.

[21] John Field, "Preface to the Reader," in Albert Peel (ed.), *The Seconde Parte of a Register* (Cambridge: Cambridge University Press, 1915), I:84.

[22] "Proclamation Ordering Deportation of Anabaptists," 22 September 1560, in Paul L. Hughes and James F. Larkin (eds.), *Tudor Royal Proclamations*, II, *The Later Tudors* (New Haven: Yale University Press, 1969):149.

[23] Edwin Sandys, *Sermons*, Parker Society (Cambridge, 1842):49.

[24] Peel, *Seconde Parte*, I:84.

[25] *MM*, 1013.

[26] This is the title of J. Stevenson's standard collection of church historical documents for the period 337-461 (rev ed., London: SPCK, 1989). What a significant

label, which says so much for the narrow preoccupations of church historians, for the period in which the Christian Church was moving from persecuted marginal status to being the persecuting religion of the Imperial establishment.

[27] *Theodosian Code*, XVI, 1.2.

[28] *Theodosian Code*, XVI, 5.40.

[29] Paul Fredericq, *Corpus Documentorum Inquisitionis Haereticae Pravitatis Neerlandicae* (Gent, 1889), I, 143, cited in Leonard Verduin: *The Anatomy of a Hybrid: A Study of Church-State Relationships* (Grand Rapids: Eerdmans, 1976): 122.

[30] Sandys, *Sermons*, 49.

[31] *MM*, 1023.

[32] *Ibid.*, 1009.

[33] Sandys, *Sermons*, 46.

[34] *MM*, 1022.

[35] *Ibid.*, 1023.

[36] See e.g. Everett Ferguson, "Inscriptions and the Origin of Infant Baptism," *Journal of Theological Studies* n.s., 30 (1979):37-46, and especially the many writings of David F. Wright, the most recent of which is "At What Ages were People Baptized in the Early Centuries?" *Studia Patristica* 30 (1997):389-394.

[37] Sandys, *Sermons*, 72.

[38] *MM*, 1012-1013.

[39] *Ibid.*, 1016.

[40] *Ibid.*, 1019.

[41] *Ibid.*, 1024.

[42] To the classic treatment (Irvin B. Horst, *The Radical Brethren: Anabaptism and the English Reformation to 1558* (Nieuwkoop: B. de Graaf, 1972) must be added the recent survey of Meic Pearse, *The Great Restoration: The Religious Radicals of the 16th and 17th Centuries* (Carlisle: Paternoster Press, 1998).

[43] For a brief statement of the Anglican perspective, see Judith Maltby: "An Anglican Looks at the Past," *Anabaptism Today* 5 (February 1994):6-8. [That we include only the Anabaptist perceptions of the Church of England, and not Judith Maltby's paper presenting Anglican perceptions, does not mean that we do not acknowledge that there were two sides to the debate, both of which have authentic insights. But in this volume we are giving preferential treatment to those who have been silenced. Eds.]

Anabaptism Tomorrow
Noel Moules

I have taught Christians across Britain for many years and there is one question I am frequently asked, "Which period of church history would you most like to have lived in?" There is never any need to pause or stop to think, the answer for me is quite simple and very clear – "today and tomorrow." Of course there are so many periods and events from the last two thousand years that entice and lure me, but it is the present and the future that are the supreme challenge and opportunity. While we build upon the incredible heritage of the past, now is always the time to discover God in fresh ways and to make a major impact. This is our *kairos* moment!

Like a ship in a storm

As we look to the future, the challenge to the Church in this country is enormous. Society and culture are involved in fundamental change – energised by individualism and consumerism, enabled by the most astonishing advances in technology, manipulated by the exploitative power of the media. Values are transient, the human story unimportant, the certainties and promises of the past an illusion. The terms "post-modern" and "post-Christian" affirm a break with what has gone before, but take us nowhere. There is existential questioning and spiritual searching everywhere; yet at the same time the majority of the population are not only unchurched but probably culturally "unchurchable."

Added to this, within the Church itself there is a watershed. Much of the Church has been washed by the wake of the charismatic movement; however, its immediate impact is all but spent. In many sectors of the Church little has been left untouched with its passing; there has been a serious shaking of foundations as well as superstructure, but to what end? Churches in historical denominations along with independent congregations have become less inhibited in worship and more spontaneous in spiritual self-expression, but now that charismatic characteristics have become part of the popular Christian ethos and the acrimonious conflicts of the early days have passed, many people are looking for something more. This fact alone reveals the shallowness of its legacy.

Across the country there has been increased networking between a whole variety of churches and groups, and there are some remarkable examples of church planting and church growth. However, rather than a growing hunger for "deepening," I believe many people have become caught up in a cycle of "happening." A taste has developed for "receiving" in preference to "being." As a result, many people are always looking for the next wave – whatever that may be; whatever that may bring. This makes them vulnerable to focusing on short-term experiences, with their fragmented theology and spiritual naivete leaving them wide open to false teaching. The hopes of many are also increasingly pinned on God sovereignly sending a revival which, with little human effort, will fill the churches and change the face of the nation. What will be the spiritual fallout if this scenario fails to unfold? For all this emphasis on experience, I nevertheless meet very few Christians with a raw excitement for God.

In contrast, there are those who are disillusioned; who feel that the spiritual promises of previous years have never been fulfilled; and their disappointment has given way to a deep sadness. For them an early freedom, joy and sense of discovery appear to have been substituted by top-down structures, where strategy is replacing spontaneity and effort has often supplanted excitement and enthusiasm. As a result, across the country, there are growing numbers of mature, experienced Christians who are no longer actively part of a local church, or only touch its fringes. They still have a deep faith and living experience of God, but have become disenfranchised disciples. To describe some of them as "post-evangelical" may perhaps define their past, but it does not connect them to a future. For them, the organised structures of the Christian community are no longer nurturing their spirituality, nor creating an environment in which their gifts can be expressed. Neither do they feel that the Church is seriously engaging with modern culture in a way that honestly grapples with the searching questions of their own hearts and of our times. It is not without significance that Christians like these are the fastest growing section of the Church in Britain today.

Nevertheless, I personally believe that the greatest weakness in the Church in Britain is with leadership. In struggling to relate living faith to changing culture, many leaders display little real sense of direction. Their lack of orientation can at times compromise their integrity. Many have become isolated, struggling to maintain both church systems and people's expectations. Others, having succumbed to the popular Christian notion that successful local church means becoming big prosperous centres of spiritual power, come under intense unspoken pressure from their congregations to be part of this experience. They are urged to become networked with other groups that are sharing in this "success syndrome." Many leaders are not leading but being driven. Along with all this comes insecurity, from which often spring authoritarian attitudes.

There is also the subtle seduction of power and the desire to be in control, which maintains hierarchical structures and fails properly to enable the community of faith to function with maturity. Most experiments with "cell-church" will fail because the cells are not genuinely empowered; authority remains centralised and they become little more than revamped house groups. Leadership weakness is also seen in superficial biblical teaching and the expectation that people will follow "party lines" in thinking. There is virtually no encouragement for individuals to reason, question and experiment for themselves and so enrich the body as a whole with divine diversity. The situation is compounded by the fact that few leaders seem aware, or prepared to admit, that anything is other than completely satisfactory. The role of leadership is vital, but the old mould of both style and thinking have got to be broken.

As the twentieth century falls behind us the challenge to the Church is serious. Apart from the concerns I have outlined above, pre-millennial tension has also exacted its toll. Few will admit to the level of expectation there has actually been. At one extreme there have been the minority, fairly certain that Jesus would return. Far greater numbers have been part of widely publicised schemes for world evangelisation or massive national church growth, all of which have fallen dramatically short of their original widely publicised objectives. Many more people just had a sense that the year 2000 should have been spiritually significant; the fact that it wasn't leaves them with the question, "Where do we go from here?" Like a ship in a storm, these are days of disappointment and often unspoken struggle with faith for many Christians.

Grasping the moment

This is where the doors open to so many wonderful possibilities! In spite of the sobering picture I have painted, many exciting things are also happening in the Church in Britain, and often in the most unexpected places. This book is an important glimpse into part of that story and promise for the future. The remarkable growth of interest in Anabaptism and the influence of its ideas are not accidental. I believe God's hand is behind it all. So many spiritual journeys, from every direction and background, are converging on an approach to the Christian faith that draws us towards the truth.

As we have seen, the term "Anabaptism" means different things to different people, yet it connects together in a common bond those touched by it. It has always held within itself a diversity of contrasting views. For me, it defines a unique ethos rather than a specific agenda. It is not so much what was experienced and experimented with in the sixteenth century, inspiring though this is, that is of primary importance. Rather it is the way in which those radical reformers rediscovered the Christian faith and approached Scripture, their ability to reach past the barriers thrown up by Christendom and to tap into the original source and character of our faith. To me, the quintessence of Anabaptism is the vision and values it confronts us with and the direction in which they call us to follow.

At its most focused, this is an encounter with the person and life of the historical Jesus, who came preaching peace. He is our model; his example, death, resurrection and the sending of the Spirit enable us to follow in his steps. Everything else flows from this irreducible central core. The word "Christocentric" recurs throughout the text of this book and that is because it is the key. It means, first and foremost, that each one of us must personally come to a place of being convinced that the new covenant experience flows from a clear commitment in discipleship to Jesus; which takes seriously his pattern of life for our own; which is prepared to practise and experiment with his hard sayings in the power of the Spirit.

Such a seemingly obvious decision for a Christian will, in reality, set us at odds with much historic – and alas contemporary – Christian thinking which has marginalised Jesus to a theological principle, rather than embracing him as the person who is our model and example.

However, I dare to believe that in God's economy one of the purposes of the charismatic movement – as of other forms of spiritual re-energising – has been to prepare the church for a liberated radical discipleship that is ignited, empowered and characterised by the presence of God and the work of the Spirit. In a Christian ethos that is looking for the next "experience," this is a cold sober choice [*metanoia*]. For the vision and values of Anabaptism to truly impact churches and secular communities, the first step must be made by individuals who are inspired by a deep joy and spontaneous freedom in Jesus.

Early Anabaptists have been described as being "neither Protestant nor Catholic." While these words make an important historical point, they also express a vital truth: the fact that there is only *one* Church. The original Anabaptists were rejected by both sides in the Reformation; our aim today is to be a catalyst in reconciliation and ecumenism. We wish to affirm the indivisible unity of the community of faith, bringing the body of Christ together. Our desire is to bridge-build and embrace everyone who names the name of Jesus, has been touched by the fire of his love and is following him. Several contributors have expressed how it is also our desire to draw deeply from the diverse streams of Christian spirituality – Celtic, Catholic, Orthodox, Protestant, ancient, modern and global – and so create a confluence of richness and reality to the glory of God. This was not possible in the historical circumstances of the sixteenth century, but I believe it is nevertheless true to the spirit of the Anabaptists. It is also essential if we are to be the one united Church God wants us to be, bold witnesses to Jesus into the future.

However, a word of warning. The increasing interest in Anabaptism across Britain itself presents a challenge. In some Christian circles people respond to new manifestations of Anabaptism with alarm, fearing that there will be new attacks on cherished Christian practices, leading to new divisions. In other Christian circles Anabaptism has positive connotations and is in danger of becoming a buzz-word. In order to sound radical, the language of some groups and individuals is merely being decorated with "Anabaptist-speak," without seriously changing their thinking or behaviour. For example, the themes of community and nonconformity appear attractive, while the subjects of non-violence and justice are ignored. The challenge to each of us is to grapple with all the issues with which the radical reformers wrestled and work out their implications in our own times. Likewise, to attempt simply to "pick'n'mix" or try to "bolt on" certain Anabaptist ideas to existing frameworks of thought is to fail to do justice to them. They must be recognised as a unique culture that ferments and changes the whole.

Closer to the centre of the network I believe there is another danger. Most of us were initially drawn towards the movement by the ideas, individuals and events of the Radical Reformation. The challenge is to be able to turn our encounter with these into tangible life-changing experiences for individuals and churches today. Solid and sustained research into all aspects of Anabaptism will always be a central task, but we must equally be conscious of the danger of the network becoming simply a historical and theological society. If the fruits of our reflection do not practically and radically change the lives of individuals, churches and secular communities across this country, then we will have missed the most incredible opportunity.

The challenges within both the Church and our culture are enormous, but I believe that the inherent Anabaptist values of thinking creatively and acting radically in the power of the Spirit can produce phenomenal results. This is not based upon some romantic view, but hard-headed experience over many years. Individuals and small groups working both within and outside existing structures can have an influence far beyond their number or their status. We must never underestimate the influence of a person whose demeanour, responses and attitudes are provocative by their unique truthfulness. Most social revolutions have spread by deeds observed or conversations shared. The power of the right word or action impacting an individual or group at exactly the right moment simply cannot be exaggerated. We should be working to change the current environment and culture of our churches and society; stimulating creative thinking, encouraging debate, provoking discussion. At every step we need to be learning from each other, sharing experiences, being humble enough to admit mistakes and childlike enough to rejoice over even small successes.

We have the chance to influence the life of the Church in this land for years ahead. It will almost certainly be "grass-roots-up" in its method, it will be gentle in its character, but it will not happen by some passive process of osmosis. If we are to grasp the moment, it will take a determined commitment on the part of each one to act boldly and single-mindedly. The question is: do we think that the themes of Anabaptism should simply be fashionable for a time, or are we convinced they point us clearly towards truth in its fundamental form?

Embracing the vision

So many Christians I meet hold the key elements of their faith like children clutching treasured fragments in their hands. Precious though these are, they have no idea how they fit into the greater scheme of things, or what that scheme might be. There is no big picture, no panoramic vision in which to place their experience, their understanding, or in which to find their identity; no paradigm within which to draw everything together and out of which can flow a sense of purpose. This is true in terms of their theology and their thinking, but it is especially true in terms of direction and ultimate destiny. I am a passionate believer that if the pathway of Christian discipleship is to lead to significant spiritual maturity and effective action, it must be orientated within the landscape of salvation history and eschatology.

Eschatology is a contentious subject. It played a significant part in the story of early Anabaptism, with some tragic results. With no consensus being held within the Church and the hype surrounding the year 2000 discrediting much populist Christian thinking, one can understand a feeling that this is a subject left well alone as we explore the challenge of Anabaptist ideas into the days ahead. I couldn't disagree more! "Last things first" – but properly understood. Hope is at the very heart of faith and yet many Christians have little sense of destiny. It is time that we grasped a biblical eschatology which clearly states there is no place for the absurd schemes and pseudo-schedules to predict "the end" which have plagued the Church over centuries. The New Testament is clear that every Christian is to be embraced by a living, life-changing hope based upon the risen Jesus. We are never to focus on particular events but only upon the person in whom everything will ultimately find its perfect consummation. Jesus' teaching calls us to live holding two themes in tension. We are to rediscover the natural rhythms of the days, the seasons and the years, finding and exploring God and life within them in a natural, relaxed way, while at the same time we look for "that day" when in Jesus everything is put right and the new heaven and new earth are established. To hold these two essential elements of Christian hope together with both quietness and excitement calls for maturity, alertness and wisdom.

History is the soil in which eschatology is rooted. Biblical history, and the subsequent story of the Church, not only has a forward look but has destiny woven into every fibre. History and eschatology are inseparably bonded, at the heart of which there is memory, story and hope. Our task is to bring this sweeping drama, with the human and divine fused together at its centre, to the Church and to the world. This, of course, runs counter to our prevailing culture which has no place for the meta-narrative, an overarching story behind human experience. To challenge this is part of our counter-cultural calling. We need to excite the Church about history, the medium of God's revelation, in which, through the work of the Spirit, meaning and distinctiveness are found. As Christians learn, and then tell and retell the stories, they will imbibe their essence, affirm their own identity in a turbulent world, and take both the memory and the message forward into the future. Telling and interpreting the story is a primary task for the local church.

In Jesus the eschatological age to come has broken into this age ahead of time, history and eternity flowing into one another. We must help Christians discover that they are the true "new age travellers," walking at the edge of time; journeying ancient paths, yet living each moment at the very forefront of existence where no one has ever lived before. Capturing the excitement of this truth and experimenting with it must be at the heart of being Church and proclaiming the gospel today and tomorrow.

For me, both history and eschatology are set into perfect perspective in the biblical vision of *shalom*. I have explained in my personal story, earlier in this book, how in the mid-1960s I stumbled upon it like a treasure in a field, and how ever since it has not only provided the framework to everything I believe, but has radicalised my whole life. In *shalom* we have the secret of the universe; the energised wholeness, integratedness and completeness, spiritual and material, which is the true character and expression of peace. It is the framework in which everything finds its place in dynamic harmony, foretasted now in the lives and actions of Christians, but ultimately expressed in the new heaven and earth. It is the fountain source from which all the values which make up God's character cascade upon creation, incarnated in Jesus and his people.

Shalom is first and foremost to do with relationships that must always be expressed in justice and peace. It is practical, tangible and measurable. It is only present when the poor are fed, clothed and sheltered, when broken relationships are mended, and when the cry of the oppressed is turned to joy because their circumstances have been put right. It is the gospel in a nutshell. It is the manifestation of the kingdom of God. There is absolutely nothing passive about *shalom*; it pulsates with energy and life. It cannot simply be reflected upon as an inspiring idea; it must be recognised and embraced as *the* dynamic agenda for the church. Christians, as disciples of Jesus, are to be nothing less than "*shalom* activists" within the world. The implications of all this we will explore in the remainder of this chapter.

Subversive spirituality

The new creation begins with women and men born anew and climaxes with the new heaven and the new earth. It stands in asymmetry with the original creation which began by creating the heavens and the earth and was completed with a couple made in the image and likeness of God. It is for this reason we must begin by focusing our attention on what it means to be a spiritual person, a godly individual, a disciple of Jesus, before we can start to consider the wider agenda.

At first glance, Christians are just like everyone else around them; their appearance, language, dress and food are no different from that of their neighbours. What is different is that they are born of the Spirit of God, they are energised by the life and powers of the age to come – all this being evidenced by the way they think, speak, act and respond within all the demands and opportunities of life. It was the disturbing depth of Jesus' being, the quality of his character and personhood, that marked him out from surrounding villagers and townsfolk, or the other mendicant rabbis of his day. If we are going to play a significant part in the story of the Church in the future, and Anabaptist perspectives are to have a real influence, it will not depend on the brilliance of our strategies (not that they are unimportant), but upon the integral quality of our lives and personalities.

We are to be people of the truth – in the foundational biblical sense of truth as being primarily the incarnation, those qualities of character which harmonise most perfectly with the character of God himself, and which liberate people to become like God. Truth as knowledge which is accurate is of course very important, but it is secondary. This is why having Jesus as our model, pattern and example is vital. We are in the process of transfiguration, experiencing the "re-reflexing" (Alan Kreider's phrase) of sanctification, discovering holistic holiness through the gentle, creative power of the Spirit. This stress on developing godliness of character after the pattern of Jesus is a primary Anabaptist emphasis.

As people of the Spirit we are called to learn to live naturally within reality in a way that destroys forever the erroneous concept of "the supernatural." Most Christians love this term and use it with enthusiasm, but unwittingly they have bought into the notion that what is real and natural is determined by what our senses can touch, taste, count and measure, and that everything outside of this is supernatural (i.e. beyond empirical evidence or rational explanation). This is perverse. True reality is rooted in the being of God himself and is the foundation of everything. So, when people speak of the supernatural, they are simply defining the current limits of their ignorance and making themselves the primary arbiters of reality. This is spiritual humanism; it disconnects spirituality from the real experience of living and makes reality subjective and temporary, because science is constantly advancing our understanding of the world.

In Jesus we are presented with the true paradigm of reality. In him we see the apparent barriers between the earthly and heavenly ripped apart forever (cf. Luke 2:8-14; Matthew 3:16; John 1:43-51). For him reality was that which had its source in his Father who was God. Miracles were for him the most natural activity, simply making happen what God wanted to happen. Jesus moved seamlessly between the visible and the invisible, demonstrating their complete integration as the true nature of reality. He also gives this tangible expression in the incarnation, where within himself humanity and divinity are fully and completely one. This in itself also becomes a sign of the essential nature of the new heaven and new earth.

I have taken the time to reflect on this because I believe it has enormous practical consequences for the Church. The popular view is not only completely false, but it dramatically distorts how people understand the way we move in faith and also presents serious problems for apologetics. In our maturity we need to become like little children again, discovering how, in the true sense, to live naturally within reality – learning to move effortlessly between the physical and the spiritual: embracing the path of the radical mystic within the world; living under an open heaven yet rooted firmly in the earthiness and struggle of the everyday life (there is no escapism), while at the same time being people through whom God mediates his life.

Freedom is a primary hallmark of the gospel, and yet in my experience it is one of the most absent qualities in the life of Christians and the churches in Britain. Spoken about in vague terms, it is always safely contained within tight theological and conceptual limits. However, Paul clearly declares, "Where the Spirit of the Lord is there is freedom" (2 Corinthians 3:17), and among my favourite passages of Scripture are the words of Jesus, "The wind blows where it chooses, and you hear the sound of it, but you do not know where it comes from or where it goes; so it is with everyone who is born of the Spirit" (John 3:8). What has gone wrong? This doesn't match experience. When the subject is addressed it is almost exclusively freedom *from*. Freedom from sin, guilt, fear – all very important, but this is just the start. What about freedom *to?*

The simple truth is that rarely in the whole story of the Church has freedom been either properly explored or satisfyingly exemplified. When it is honestly examined it scares most leaders and teachers in the Church. Fear of the libertine leads them to hedge freedom with law, however subtly. They stress external restraints rather than internal spiritual moral structures, and so miss the treasure completely. This touches the very essence of what the new covenant is all about. Freedom is a huge undiscovered territory waiting to be encountered; the challenge is incredibly exciting!

Again our example is Jesus; everything about him breathed freedom. He was so natural in his behaviour, sensitive to others, and yet he refused to conform to anything which inhibited the character of God in his life or actions. You never knew what he would do next, he often shocked bystanders and his disciples, yet everything he did was consistent. He would break the Sabbath law with impunity and yet submit to paying the Temple tax so as not to offend people unnecessarily! He both delighted and scandalised onlookers, and of course terrified and enraged the religious political establishment. It was his freedom that nailed him to the cross. C. S. Lewis captures the freedom of Jesus perfectly when in the Narnia stories it is said of Aslan (Jesus), "He is wild but he is good."

True freedom has at its heart creativity, wisdom and the power of the Spirit – like jewels that balance the movement of an intricate timepiece. It is the ability to see what most people are blind to, bringing together elements that others would never connect, suggesting perspectives that are risky and disturbing, finding simplicity in complexity; and so much more. Sensing the will of God, the true nature of circumstances, the needs and motivations of others and acting to entwine them in a way that enriches everything; judging behaviour by its consequences rather than how it exploits opportunity; having the courage to stand firm at enormous personal cost; living with a poise that draws respect and yet creates curiosity and sometimes offence – all this characterises true freedom. I have long struggled to find a phrase to capture the excitement of Christian freedom. The only one that gets close is to describe a disciple of Jesus as a "messianic anarchist" – with the emphasis on "messianic."

The Anabaptists were absolutely right to see non-violence at the very centre of discipleship; it is the keystone to Jesus' moral teaching; it is the practical outworking of *shalom* as the radical gentleness of compassionate love. Our task is not simply to get peace back on to the Christian agenda, but to get people to see that peace *is* the agenda! When *shalom* becomes both the vision and foundation within which we stand, and its practical expression in love, nurturing, non-violence, gentleness, peacemaking, justice, mediation, reconciliation, creation sensitivity and so much more are at the centre of our action, reactions and lifestyle – the impact will be significant. The obstacles are substantial. The majority of Christians either do not believe, or have never considered, that the teaching of Jesus precludes any act of violence in any circumstance whatsoever. Nor do they even think it is of much spiritual importance. The task of consciousness-raising and challenge is huge.

Added to this, however, I feel that among those already committed to peace, their thinking has been shaped by years of responding to the global nuclear threat of the Cold War. While international instability today is greater, it is perceived that the likelihood of war is less, and so interest dissipates. Energies have turned to mediation and reconciliation work, which is wonderful and vital. However, when I look at the whole issue of Christian peace thinking in this country, I feel there is something vital missing at the very roots. I ask myself why there are so few books, easily available in popular style, that set out clearly the Christian peace position? I want to see people vigorously engaging in the pacifism/war debate, but on its own it is in danger of becoming merely theoretical. We live in a culture in which there is violence at every level, most of it subtle and pernicious, some of it overt and extreme. The radical gentleness of Jesus demands that we begin by addressing it in our deepest attitudes and emotions and from there work out to remove violence from every relationship and situation we encounter. Only from this position can we ever hope to handle either the violent street attack or a global threat in the style of Jesus.

The days ahead demand a subversive spirituality that confronts popular Christian and secular assumptions, disciples of Jesus who are dissidents, not only in society but in the Church. Their strong winsomeness will provoke people to think about the truth. Confronting attitudes in a way that produces "*shalom* shock" will in the process set people free and excite them to discover God in Jesus for themselves.

Church as conspiracy

I really do love the word "conspiracy"; it means "breathing together." What a perfect description of church! Imagine a dark cellar, faces lit only by the flickering light of a storm lantern at the centre of an old oak table; everyone is breathing quietly together as they plot and plan excitedly. God himself is part of the group. How wonderful, and how absolutely Anabaptist! As Christians, we are committed to the complete and total overthrow of the status quo and are working for the liberating in-breaking of God's perfect rule; churches are the agents in the field.

Church is people, lives interwoven as a community of mutuality, sharing and networking; a body, the body of Christ. The Quaker affirmation has never been surpassed: "a society of friends." These are aspirations frequently voiced but rarely realised because other church emphases are usually thought more important, and friendship is considered a luxury. Love, support and nurture are what enable members to grow and outsiders to be drawn in. This is where the conspiracy is born. This is a primary Anabaptist principle that must be at the heart of how we develop and influence local church into the future.

Flowing naturally from this is the question of leadership styles and models. The top-down tendency which is re-emerging in many churches gives rise to concern; it is simple and practical but it is not godly. We need to be pointing in fresh directions. Leadership is vital, but as "servant-enablers," creating the environment in which the gifts, ability and potential of the whole body can flourish. Its decisions should emphasise consensus. Its form must express both plurality and gender balance. The situation of women in leadership in many British churches today is worse than a decade ago. The ordination of Anglican women gives an illusion of progress everywhere but camouflages the reality in many churches. Most men who once argued against women in leadership now say it is no problem, but they do little that is significant to advance or empower them. In some churches women once eager to serve and lead now feel their lack of development is due to their own spiritual inadequacy. The fact is that male attitudes and control have hardly changed, a reality often disguised by tokenism. Some local churches are awash with people with deep feelings of guilt and failure reinforced by styles of teaching and leadership. It is vital that we confront this directly. It is vital we create the space for people to question, doubt, discover and share. The certainties and dogmatism of much of the Church simply does not allow this. We can encourage this without feeling threatened and be much stronger because of it. In contrast, we must become communities that envelop people in God's extravagant grace and the joy of freedom.

The secret of local church is not in its structure but in its ethos and values. The myth of "the New Testament church pattern" must be exploded. The biblical text presents only the broadest principles which can, and should, be expressed in a multitude of different ways. What should local churches be like? The simple answer is that there is no simple answer! By their very nature they should have great variety in style, structure and self-expression while holding the faith in common. They must express the varied experiences of God shared by the congregation. They should be shaped by the diverse needs, character and cultures of the group, plus the particular demands of their geographical and social circumstances. Experiment and creativity is all-important! A test on visiting any local church should be that it is a place where every Christian feels at home while at the same time being intrigued and taken by surprise.

Most of our work in bringing Anabaptist vision and values into church life will be by endeavouring to radicalise existing congregations within every tradition, and of course learning much from them in return. However, planting new local communities of faith must be a high priority. This presents many questions. Should these churches be autonomous or networked? Should they be referred to as Anabaptist churches or "Peace churches," or be more subtly named? Should we be looking to see more Mennonite and Hutterian congregations established, drawing from their deep repository of experience and tradition? We must have the creative courage to experiment with completely different ways of being church as appropriate; connecting with people culturally incapable of connecting with established patterns; enabling those who are disenfranchised to become part of the body again. Whatever choices we make, the test will be that people are able to see clearly for themselves local congregations or groups where the Anabaptist ethos is making its contribution to a living and life-changing reality. In working for change, we must remember that the power of the role model is vital, whether it is the life of an individual or a way of expressing church. Most people need something to see as an example. Theory and ideas are one thing, a practical example another. This is how people understand, learn and find the confidence to change.

As the community of faith gathers together, what takes place is so important. Worship is life, and it is in the liturgy that this can be shared. This is where we "breathe together." It must be relaxed and natural, dynamic, creative, contemplative and joyous, drawing from traditions east and west, north and south, past and present, local and global. Again it will actively involve the whole congregation, adults and children, with leaders serving as enablers, giving room for all the gifts of the Spirit to be expressed and each individual to contribute. Breaking bread, the "peace meal," must be at the heart of the gathering.

In some traditions this is already central and sacred, while in others it is unimportant and marginalised. The context of the meal must be rediscovered; the bread and wine rescued from its isolation simply as a religious rite and eaten with real appetite feeding body and spirit, a place of intimate divine encounter, but also the opportunity for the hungry and the stranger to be fed.

There is also of course the issue of baptism. It is not enough simply to debate between the issues of infant baptism or adult baptism. Much believers' baptism has become little more than endorsing local church membership and fails to be the powerful spiritual encounter and radical break from the past into the future that we find in the New Testament. No tradition gets off lightly here! I am a passionate Anabaptist but, apart from being convinced that baptism must be on personal confession of faith, I find myself one with paedobaptists when it comes to children and the Church – though many of them need to be more radical in practice. Rarely do those who practise believers' baptism take Jesus' teaching on children seriously (cf. Matthew 18:1-10; Mark 9:36-37; 10:13-16 etc.). He makes it clear that they are in the kingdom of God until, and unless, they choose otherwise. Children born into Christian families are neither "potential church members," nor "the church of tomorrow"; they are at the very heart of the church today. They can be active participants in worship and breaking bread from the beginning. Then when they are mature enough publicly to affirm their commitment to Jesus in baptism, they can do so, endorsing all that has gone before. If we take the teaching of Jesus about children seriously, local church simply cannot function as it usually does. These are some of his hard sayings that I feel most Anabaptists have failed to grapple with satisfactorily.

Disciples are people who are learning together. Therefore, thinking and teaching, discussing and discovering, must be foundational to local church life. Studying the Scriptures honestly and applying them to life courageously was a defining feature of the early Anabaptists, and must mark us out as well. We live in a national culture that is ignorant of the biblical story; we live in a church environment in which theological understanding is shallow. There is a major task here. Central to this is Bible interpretation; this is the rock from which church life is hewn but also the stone of stumbling between different traditions. We must explore together what distinctive contributions the Anabaptists made to the practice of hermeneutics (as Stuart Murray's important work has done), and then act upon them. It must be a community exercise in which everyone has the opportunity to share their prayerful reflections. The work of the scholar and the expert is valued, along with the insight of the homemaker or shop worker. Together practical and spiritual understanding is sought, truth explored, conclusions experimented with and the consequences reflected upon. The way in which ordinary men and women in the early Anabaptist movement were able to stand fearlessly before the local magistrate and clergy, on trial for their lives, and give a clear and confident exposition of Scripture and defence of their faith is a spirit and quality we must recapture.

A primary challenge to Anabaptism tomorrow is the need to re-examine the nature of the gospel we proclaim. I am deeply concerned as to the character of the message that is preached in many churches and the basis of the response that people are making. Evangelism is totally "good news," proclaiming the gospel of peace. Sin is something that is quite naturally revealed when a person is faced up with the truth of God's character in the power of the Spirit. Atonement is making enemies into friends by dealing with offences and discovering forgiveness. We never see Jesus using guilt to manipulate anyone; they either respond or they don't. If they turn away, he does not shout condemnation after them; he is simply sad at their rejection of grace. We urgently need new models of evangelism. Not least because evangelism is not simply an offer of salvation, but rather a call to discipleship, the challenge to be a witness to the truth. The call is to a radical lifestyle, not just a set of beliefs. It is the experience of a genuine freedom, joy and peace that is neither "easy believe-ism" nor an encounter with guilt or legalism.

The gospel impels us into the real world. We must connect with people where they are and with the issues they are facing. Two important areas of focus are ethics and apologetics; this is where the real questions and perplexities are to be found. People should not simply be confronted with dogmatic answers; this is the nature of neither life nor truth. They want to work sensitively with someone towards a solution with the aid of gentle questions and intriguing wisdom. This is the way that Jesus engaged with people and we should follow his example. Of course, there is a place at times for challenge and confrontation; Jesus was a master at this! Creative dialogue in an atmosphere of committed friendship, with a lifestyle that confirms our words, is the key that leads towards the challenge and choice of becoming a disciple of Jesus.

Our mission is to people, but people within the social-political environment that shapes all our lives. We bring good news to the poor, but we must also ask, "Why are they poor?" We reach out to prisoners, but we have to ask, "Is this justice?" There is the huge urban challenge of our cities with both their power and their deprivation. Our task is to build church, but also to confront the structures in which lives are enmeshed. If the gospel does not have a social impact as well as a personal one it doesn't match the biblical pattern. This of course leads to the question of church/state relations which continues to be an area of debate. As Christians, we are to be an uncoerced people, while at the same time being salt and light and working for justice and peace. Some Christians are eager to see biblical standards enshrined in law; rather, we should rejoice in the privilege of living in a secular multicultural society. We see law as limited to providing protection to the vulnerable and a bulwark against injustice on principles all fair-minded people can agree upon. We work within and without the system for what is right, but also for freedom. We know that the moral and spiritual qualities that uniquely make us Christians come from a free commitment of faith and the power of the Spirit in our lives and can never be legislated for.

The Anabaptist conspiracy is here. Nothing must remain the same, neither ourselves, the Church, nor society at large. We must be both a thorn and a balm. The opportunities are astonishing if only we will take them; but remember – we can miss them! There certainly never has been a more exciting time to be a Christian. If we get to grips with the vision and values of *shalom* as disciples of Jesus, both today and tomorrow can be different; let's go for it!

The Editors' Stories

Coming Home to Anabaptism
Stuart Murray, London

Stuart Murray is Oasis Director of Church Planting and Evangelism at Spurgeon's College, a tutor on the college's MTh course in Baptist and Anabaptist Studies, and editor of Anabaptism Today.

I am never sure how to respond when asked to identify myself with a denominational label. I grew up in a Brethren family. I was educated at a school with an Anglican chaplaincy. I came to personal faith through a church with Methodist roots. I have been deeply influenced by the charismatic movement. I have planted a house church. And I currently teach in a Baptist training college. I seem to be a hybrid. But since discovering the Anabaptist tradition about fifteen years ago, while involved in urban church planting, I have chosen increasingly to identify myself with it. Like most Anabaptists in the British Isles, I have no lineal roots to this tradition, but it is where I feel at home.

In the mid-1980s, as an urban church planter involved in a growing church in the London borough of Tower Hamlets, I came to realise that my evangelical background and more recent charismatic experience had not adequately prepared me for mission and ministry in East London. Though grateful for this background and continuing to draw on it, I was struggling with issues of powerlessness, injustice, alienation, division and the irrelevance of much church life in an urban context. Searching for new resources, I discovered Anabaptism. But what on earth could the Anabaptist tradition contribute to urban ministry in the late twentieth century? The only contemporary Anabaptists I was aware of were Mennonite farmers or rural Hutterite communities. But as I read Mennonite and then earlier Anabaptist writings, I discovered many themes that I found deeply relevant to church planting in inner London.

Among these were the empowering of uneducated Christians; the implications of starting with Jesus when reading the Bible; the importance of building community rather than holding meetings; the centrality of themes such as kingdom and peace; and the new perspective on mission that comes from rejecting the notion of a Christian nation. A critical moment for me was listening to a Mennonite pastor reflecting on the subject of "power evangelism" and commenting that unless this is set in the right context it may serve only to justify more powerfully than ever an unjust status quo. This comment, in a hotel room in Falmouth far from my urban context, helped clarify for me the vital connection between charismatic experience and social radicalism.

I have continued to study Anabaptism and to explore such themes. From 1989 to 1992 I took time out from active ministry to engage in doctoral research and chose to delve further into Anabaptism. The question which I explored in my thesis was: "Why did the Reformers and Anabaptists agree about the authority of the Bible but disagree fundamentally about how to interpret it and apply its teachings in the areas of ethics and ecclesiology?" I became – and remain – convinced that Christendom had damaged and distorted biblical interpretation and that the Anabaptists' approach was liberating. Since then, as I have continued to study sporadically, I have discovered that the Anabaptist movement was preceded by many other marginalised groups who approached the Bible in similar ways and who held similar convictions and values – a radical alternative church history.

And I have found many others, from all kinds of backgrounds, for whom this tradition offers fresh hope and vision. Friendships made in an Anabaptist Study Group in London during the 1980s were life-giving and led naturally to the development of the Anabaptist Network, which I chair, and the publication of *Anabaptism Today*, which I have edited since its inception. I have also been involved in the development of an MTh course in Baptist and Anabaptist Studies at Spurgeon's College in London, which offers an opportunity for those interested in the Anabaptist tradition to study it in depth.

I don't believe that the Anabaptist tradition provides everything we need for mission, discipleship and church life in the coming years. I continue to consider myself a hybrid, with friends in many traditions.

I want to drink from many streams. But I remain convinced that Anabaptism has a vital contribution to make. In common with many others, I feel that I have come home to Anabaptism and have found here a vision that inspires me and a way of following Jesus that makes sense in a post-Christendom society.

Coming out as Anabaptists
Alan Kreider, Oxford

Alan Kreider is Director of the Centre for the Study of Christianity and Culture, Regent's Park College, Oxford. Since 1974 he has been a missionary with the Mennonite Board of Mission. He and Eleanor Kreider have shared many dimensions of their ministry; they often speak together.

When did we first hear the word "Anabaptist"? Neither Eleanor nor I remembers, but we must have been young. We grew up in Mennonite families and churches in Northern Indiana in which Anabaptism was a buzz word. Eleanor studied church history with the father of the "Anabaptist Vision," Harold Bender; and that same Harold Bender once cornered me, stocking shelves at a super-market, to suggest I consider going into the ministry. So we knew the Anabaptist approach to Christian discipleship was a "good thing," but neither of us was overtly affected by it. Eleanor was preparing to be an organist and music teacher; I was intending to be a historian specialising in Tudor England. It was to pursue these interests that, in 1966, we came to England. To our surprise, it was there that we met an expression of Anabaptism that spoke to us deeply – the community of shared life and worship among the staff and students in the London Mennonite Centre.

It was the Viet Nam war that turned me towards Anabaptism. Between 1970 and 1972, while teaching history at Goshen College, Indiana, I taught a course on "Comparative Revolutions" which posed the issues sharply. In a world full of manifest injustice, how could I, a

COMING HOME

rich Westerner, continue to view myself as a Christian? I concluded that I could do so only if Jesus was more radical than the violent revolutionaries (John Howard Yoder helped me see this) and if I was willing to follow Jesus unconditionally. I decided to become, first of all, an Anabaptist/Mennonite Christian, but what this meant for the future was not clear.

A research grant brought us back to England for two more years. We found ourselves learning a great deal from English Christians, especially from Anglicans about liturgy and from Evangelicals about prayer and small group Bible study. I began to get speaking invitations. After one of these, in 1973, I suddenly had a loud thought: "I'm the first Anabaptist to have a chance to speak publicly in England since 1575." This underscored the sense that both of us had that God was calling us to become missionaries at the London Mennonite Centre, in Highgate, North London.

We were not prepared for our new ministry. Neither of us was trained theologically, so we had to learn a lot from hard experience and from others, especially from Jim Punton, a dynamic Church of Scotland Bible teacher who loved Jesus and despaired of Christendom. "Why don't you talk more about Anabaptism?" he asked us. "It's your thing." We had a cautious sense of the importance of Anabaptist insights. We had read John Yoder's *The Politics of Jesus* and tried to come to grips with it. In 1975, we commemorated the 400th anniversary of the burning of Anabaptist martyrs in London by placing a notice in *The Times*.

But most of the time, we didn't talk about Anabaptism – even, to our regret, in the Wood Green Mennonite Church, which we helped to found and lead. We talked about Jesus, radical discipleship community and Christian peacemaking, but not much about Anabaptism. When people outside our church mentioned Anabaptism, it was a pejorative: "That's an Anabaptist argument" was a sufficient put-down to rubbish an argument by classification. It seemed dangerous to be an Anabaptist.

So we, as agreeable and rather timid folk, sought common ground with other Christians. We learned from friends at Post Green Community in Dorset, the sisters of Grandchamp in Switzerland, and friends across the country and beyond. When we were asked to speak, we concentrated on great integrative themes such as *Shalom*;

for us there could be no separation of salvation from justice or prayer from peacemaking. We pointed to Jesus as the focus of our faith and as the one who calls us to walk as he walked. We opposed nuclear arms, arguing on grounds that we believed both pacifists and just war advocates could accept. Occasionally someone would say to us, "That's an interesting approach. Where do you get ideas like that?" But only slowly did we get the sense that we should talk explicitly about Anabaptism.

What pushed us to become more overtly Anabaptist? One thing was reading *Martyrs Mirror*. I chose this for a Baptist Historical Society lecture in 1981, and reading the accounts and letters of the martyrs moved me as no treatises on Anabaptist theology had ever done. The other thing that helped us to "come out" was meeting English friends who were excited by what Anabaptism had to offer to mission in contemporary England. The major impetus was the formation of an Anabaptist Study Group, which drew in people who soon became important to us, the thinking of the group, and the bracing discussions that we had together.

In 1991 when we were about to leave London for a four-year stint in Manchester, the Anabaptist Network was launched. Interest exceeded our imagination, and we have since then been working with others to give expression to this vision. For us this has meant travelling, making friends, and supporting others in their faith journeys. We have learned a lot about how networks develop. We have seen the very special impact that, in God's purposes, some people have upon other people. We have been amazed to watch the *Workshop* courses and to participate in them. People from many parts of the British Isles have discovered that, without leaving their denominations, they have entered networks of solidarity in an Anabaptist-type Christianity. "Hyphenated Anabaptism" has been about friendship as much as theology!

Since coming to Oxford in 1995, the two of us have continued developing our own characteristic themes and roles: for Eleanor, worship as a multi-voiced reality, leading to passionate commitment to the Lord and one another; for me, the "peace church," in which God re-reflexes us to respond to the world not just with a "no" to war but with a Jesus-accented "yes" to peacemaking. Occasionally we have caught glimpses of the uses that God may be making of the

Anabaptist Network. All of us in it are playing small but essential parts in the greater drama that God is writing. We are not the whole show; other actors are important. But the re-emergence, after almost 500 years, of the repressed European Anabaptist past is bringing essential gifts for the future of Christianity's mission. We only know bits of this; others, still latent in the Anabaptist story, are there to be re-awakened. But we sense that, in a post-Christendom world in which people are bored with Christianity and certain that nothing new can be expected from the church, Anabaptist insights point to areas of experiment and discovery that are profoundly hopeful.

Anabaptist Resources in Britain

Anabaptist Network

14 Shepherd's Hill, Highgate, London N6 5AQ
Tel: 020 8340 8775; Fax: 020 8341 6807; E-mail: an@menno.org.uk
The network arranges conferences, sponsors local study groups, distributes resources for studying Anabaptism, provides an annual newsletter and, three times a year, a prayer diary.

Anabaptism Today

23 Barnes Close, Farnborough, Hants GU14 7JA Tel: 01252 545902. Published three times a year, this is the journal of the Anabaptist Network, offering articles on historical themes and contemporary discipleship in the radical tradition. Index and most back issues are available.

In February 1997, we published a special introductory issue of *Anabaptism Today* (Issue 14) that provides a summary of the history and distinctive practices of the Anabaptists. A complimentary copy of this issue is available on request.

London Mennonite Centre

14 Shepherd's Hill, Highgate, London N6 5AQ
Tel: 0181 340 8775; Fax: 0181 341 6807;
Webpage:www.menno.org.uk; E-mail: lmc@menno.org.uk
Standing within the Anabaptist tradition, the staff and community of the London Mennonite Centre seek to cultivate Christian discipleship as a way of life. The Centre serves as a catalyst and resource through its library, prayer hut, teaching programmes, ministry of hospitality, book service (Metanoia), and conflict transformation programme (Bridge Builders).

Metanoia Book Service

14 Shepherd's Hill, Highgate, London N6 5AQ Tel:020 8340 8775; Fax: 020 8341 6807;
E-mail: metanoia@menno.org.uk
Metanoia, a book service located at the London Mennonite Centre, offers mail order services to individuals and groups who are seeking

Anabaptist and Christian discipleship resources. In addition to titles related to Anabaptist History and Theology, Metanoia offers a special selection of books on such topics as Christian Peacemaking, Conflict Transformation and Mediation, Mission, the Church, Biblical Studies, and Spirituality. Catalogues and special orders are available upon request.

Bridge Builders

14 Shepherd's Hill, Highgate, London N6 5AQ Tel: 020 8340 8775; Fax 020 8341 6807;
E-mail: bridgebuilders@menno.org.uk
Bridge Builders, a service of the London Mennonite Centre, aims to inspire Christians with a vision for making peace as an intrinsic part of faithfully following Jesus. Bridge Builders offers a service to help transform conflicts in British churches and their denominations by providing training in understanding and handling church conflict, and through facilitation and mediation for transforming specific conflicts. Bridge Builders is committed to empowering congregations and denominational structures to prepare proactively for, and to respond creatively to conflict.

The Bruderhof

The Bruderhof is a Christian community movement of approximately 2500 men, women and children who follow New Testament teachings including non-violence, love of neighbour, mutual service, purity and faithfulness in marriage. Like the early Christians, Bruderhof members forsake private property, voluntarily pool money and possessions and give time and talents wherever they are needed. The Bruderhof community and its activities are primarily supported by the operations of its own businesses. While many descendants of the original Bruderhof remain in the community, any adult seeking a simple life of service following the teachings of Jesus Christ may seek membership. All members work without pay and share a life commitment to brotherly/sisterly relationships with their co-workers. Each year Bruderhof communities host thousands of visitors of all backgrounds and creeds.

There are two Bruderhofs in England:

Darvell Bruderhof: Robertsbridge, East Sussex TN32 5DR (Tel 01580 883344; Free Phone 0800 269048; Fax 01580 883319)

Beech Grove Bruderhof: Nonington, Kent CT15 4HH (Tel:01304 842980)

Plough Publishing House

Darvell Bruderhof, Robertsbridge, East Sussex TN32 5DR (Tel 01580 883344; Free Phone UK 0800 269048; Fax 01580 883319)
The Plough Publishing House publishes and sells books on radical Christian discipleship, community, marriage, parenting, social justice and the spiritual life. A small periodical, *The Plough*, brings articles on current issues the mainstream media tend to ignore and reflective pieces on personal and societal transformation.

MTh in Baptist and Anabaptist Studies

Validated by the University of Wales and offered by Spurgeon's College, 189 South Norwood Hill, London SE25 6DJ (tel: 0181 653 0850; fax: 0181 771 0959; e-mail: enquiries@spurgeons.ac.uk)
An opportunity to study Anabaptist and English Baptist history and convictions. The course can be studied through a seminar programme at Spurgeon's College. It is also available as an Open Learning course with no attendance requirements, so can be studied anywhere in the world.

Workshop

104 Townend Lane, Deepcar, Sheffield S36 2TS (tel: 0114 288 8816; fax: 0114 288 8817; e-mail : anvil@dial.pipex.com)
Workshop is a Christian discipleship and leadership training programme for people with busy lives who nonetheless wish to study all the major aspects of their faith in an inclusive manner. It runs one weekend a month for eleven months drawing participants from the whole range of Christian backgrounds and experience. It is committed to applying their faith to the challenges of today drawing on firm biblical roots.

Recommended Books

Most books on Anabaptism and related subjects are published in North America. These can be consulted in the library of the London Mennonite Centre. Books in print can be ordered from Metanoia Book Service or Plough Publishing House (at the addresses above). We offer here a short list of books published recently in Britain which draw on Anabaptist perspectives:

Clement, C J: *Religious Radicalism in England, 1535-1565* (Carlisle: Paternoster Press, 1996)

Jones, Keith: *A Believing Church* (Didcot: Baptist Union, 1998)

Kreider, Alan: *Journey Towards Holiness* (Basingstoke: Marshalls, 1986)

Kreider, Alan: *Worship and Evangelism in Pre-Christendom* (Cambridge: Grove Books, 1995)

Kreider, Eleanor: *Given for You: A Fresh Look at Communion* (Leicester: IVP, 1998)

Murray, Stuart: *Church Planting: Laying Foundations* (Carlisle: Paternoster, 1998)

Murray, Stuart: *Explaining Church Discipline* (Tonbridge: Sovereign World, 1995)

Pearse, Meic: *The Great Restoration: The Religious Radicals of the 16th and 17th Centuries* (Carlisle: Paternoster, 1998)

Pearse, Meic: *Who's Feeding Whom?* (Carlisle: Paternoster, 1997)

Wright, Nigel: *Challenge to Change* (Eastbourne: Kingsway, 1991)

Wright, Nigel: *The Radical Kingdom* (Eastbourne: Kingsway, 1986)

Wright, Nigel: *The Radical Evangelical* (London: SPCK, 1996)

Video: Rediscovering Anabaptism

Interviews with members of the Anabaptist Network, several of whose stories are included in this book, who talk about central themes in Anabaptism and how these have been significant for them and their churches. Available from Metanoia Book Service (at the address above).

About Pandora Press

Pandora Press is a small, independently owned press dedicated to making available modestly priced books that deal with Anabaptist, Mennonite, and Believers Church topics, both historical and theological. We welcome comments from our readers.

Edna Schroeder Thiessen and Angela Showalter, *A Life Displaced: A Mennonite Woman's Flight from War-Torn Poland*
(Kitchener: Pandora Press, 2000; co-published with Herald Press)
> Softcover, xii, 218pp. ISBN 0-9685543-2-6
> $20.00 U.S./$24.00 Canadian. Postage: $4.00 U.S./$5.00 Can.
[A true story: moving, richly-detailed, told with candor and courage]

Stuart Murray, *Biblical Interpretation in the Anabaptist Tradition*
(Kitchener: Pandora Press, 2000; co-published with Herald Press)
> Softcover, 310pp. ISBN 0-9685543-3-4
> $28.00 U.S./$32.00 Canadian. Postage: $4.00 U.S./$5.00 Can.
[How Anabaptists read the Bible; considerations for today's church]

Apocalypticism and Millennialism, ed. by Loren L. Johns
(Kitchener: Pandora Press, 2000; co-published with Herald Press)
> Softcover, 419pp; Scripture and name indeces
> ISBN 0-9683462-9-4
> $37.50 U.S./$44.00 Canadian. Postage: $5.00 U.S./$6.00 Can.
[A clear, careful, and balanced collection: pastoral and scholarly]

Later Writings by Pilgram Marpeck and his Circle. Volume 1: The Exposŭ, A Dialogue and Marpeck's Response to Caspar Schwenckfeld
Translated by Walter Klaassen, Werner Packull, and John Rempel
(Kitchener: Pandora Press, 1999; co-published with Herald Press)
> Softcover, 157pp. ISBN 0-9683462-6-X
> $20.00 U.S./$23.00 Canadian. Postage: $4.00 U.S./$5.00 Can.
[Previously untranslated writings by Marpeck and his Circle]

John Driver, *Radical Faith. An Alternative History of the Christian Church,* edited by Carrie Snyder.
(Kitchener: Pandora Press, 1999; co-published with Herald Press)
> Softcover, 334pp. ISBN 0-9683462-8-6
> $32.00 U.S./$35.00 Canadian. Postage: $5.00 U.S./$6.00 Can.
[A history of the church as it is seldom told – from the margins]

C. Arnold Snyder, *From Anabaptist Seed. The Historical Core of Anabaptist-Related Identity*
(Kitchener: Pandora Press, 1999; co-published with Herald Press)
    Softcover, 53pp.; discussion questions. ISBN 0-9685543-0-X
    $5.00 U.S./$6.25 Canadian. Postage: $2.00 U.S./$2.50 Can.
[Ideal for group study, commissioned by Mennonite World Conf.]
    Also available in Spanish translation: *De Semilla Anabautista*,
    from Pandora Press only.

John D. Thiesen, *Mennonite and Nazi? Attitudes Among Mennonite Colonists in Latin America, 1933-1945.*
(Kitchener: Pandora Press, 1999; co-published with Herald Press)
    Softcover, 330pp., 2 maps, 24 b/w illustrations, bibliography,
    index. ISBN 0-9683462-5-1
    $25.00 U.S./$28.00 Canadian. Postage: $4.00 U.S./$5.00 Can.
    [Careful and objective study of an explosive topic]

Lifting the Veil, a translation of *Aus meinem Leben: Erinnerungen von J.H. Janzen.* Ed. by Leonard Friesen; trans. by Walter Klaassen
(Kitchener: Pandora Press, 1998; co-pub. with Herald Press).
    Softcover, 128pp.; 4pp. of illustrations. ISBN 0-9683462-1-9
    $12.50 U.S./$14.00 Canadian. Postage: $4.00 U.S. and Can.
[Memoir, confession, critical observation of Mennonite life in Russia]

Leonard Gross, *The Golden Years of the Hutterites*, rev. ed.
(Kitchener: Pandora Press, 1998; co-pub. with Herald Press).
    Softcover, 280pp., index. ISBN 0-9683462-3-5
    $22.00 U.S./$25.00 Canadian. Postage: $4.00 U.S./$5.00 Can.
[Classic study of early Hutterite movement, now available again]

The Believers Church: A Voluntary Church, ed. by William H. Brackney
(Kitchener: Pandora Press, 1998; co-published with Herald Press).
    Softcover, viii, 237pp., index. ISBN 0-9683462-0-0
    $25.00 U.S./$27.50 Canadian. Postage: $4.00 U.S./$5.00 Can.
[Papers from the 12th Believers Church Conference, Hamilton, ON]

An Annotated Hutterite Bibliography, compiled by Maria H. Krisztinkovich, ed. by Peter C. Erb (Kitchener, Ont.: Pandora Press, 1998). (Ca. 2,700 entries) 312pp., cerlox bound, electronic, or both.
ISBN (paper) 0-9698762-8-9/(disk) 0-9698762-9-7
$15.00 each, U.S. and Canadian. Postage: $6.00 U.S. and Can.
[The most extensive bibliography on Hutterite literature available]

Jacobus ten Doornkaat Koolman, *Dirk Philips. Friend and Colleague of Menno Simons*, trans. W. E. Keeney, ed. C. A. Snyder (Kitchener: Pandora Press, 1998; co-pub. with Herald Press).
Softcover, xviii, 236pp., index. ISBN: 0-9698762-3-8
$23.50 U.S./$28.50 Canadian. Postage: $4.00 U.S./$5.00 Can.
[The definitive biography of Dirk Philips, now available in English]

Sarah Dyck, ed./tr., *The Silence Echoes: Memoirs of Trauma & Tears* (Kitchener: Pandora Press, 1997; co-published with Herald Press).
Softcover, xii, 236pp., 2 maps. ISBN: 0-9698762-7-0
$17.50 U.S./$19.50 Canadian. Postage: $4.00 U.S./$5.00 Can.
[First person accounts of life in the Soviet Union, trans. from German]

Wes Harrison, *Andreas Ehrenpreis and Hutterite Faith and Practice* (Kitchener: Pandora Press, 1997; co-published with Herald Press).
Softcover, xxiv, 274pp., 2 maps, index. ISBN 0-9698762-6-2
$26.50 U.S./$32.00 Canadian. Postage: $4.00 U.S./$5.00 Can.
[First biography of this important seventeenth century Hutterite leader]

C. Arnold Snyder, *Anabaptist History and Theology: Revised Student Edition* (Kitchener: Pandora Press, 1997; co-pub. Herald Press).
Softcover, xiv, 466pp., 7 maps, 28 illustrations, index, bibliography. ISBN 0-9698762-5-4
$35.00 U.S./$38.00 Canadian. Postage: $5.00 U.S./$6.00 Can.
[Abridged, rewritten edition for undergraduates and the non-specialist]

Nancey Murphy, *Reconciling Theology and Science: A Radical Reformation Perspective* (Kitchener, Ont.: Pandora Press, 1997; co-pub. Herald Press).
Softcover, x, 103pp., index. ISBN 0-9698762-4-6
$14.50 U.S./$17.50 Canadian. Postage: $3.50 U.S./$4.00 Can.
[Exploration of the supposed conflict between Christianity and Science]

C. Arnold Snyder and Linda A. Huebert Hecht, eds, *Profiles of Anabaptist Women: Sixteenth Century Reforming Pioneers* (Waterloo, Ont.: Wilfrid Laurier University Press, 1996).

> Softcover, xxii, 442pp. ISBN: 0-88920-277-X
> $28.95 U.S. or Canadian. Postage: $5.00 U.S./$6.00 Can.

[Biographical sketches of more than 50 Anabaptist women; a first]

The Limits of Perfection: A Conversation with J. Lawrence Burkholder 2nd ed., with a new epilogue by J. Lawrence Burkholder, Rodney Sawatsky and Scott Holland, eds. (Kitchener: Pandora Press, 1996).

> Softcover, x, 154pp. ISBN 0-9698762-2-X
> $10.00 U.S./$13.00 Canadian. Postage: $2.00 U.S./$3.00 Can.

[J.L. Burkholder on his life experiences; eight Mennonites respond]

C. Arnold Snyder, *Anabaptist History and Theology: An Introduction* (Kitchener: Pandora Press, 1995).   ISBN 0-9698762-0-3

> Softcover, x, 434pp., 6 maps, 29 illustrations, index, bibliography.
> $35.00 U.S./$38.00 Canadian. Postage: $5.00 U.S./$6.00 Can.

[Comprehensive survey; unabridged version, fully documented]

C. Arnold Snyder, *The Life and Thought of Michael Sattler* (Scottdale: Herald Press, 1984).

> Hardcover, viii, 260pp. ISBN 0-8361-1264-4
> $10.00 U.S./$12.00 Canadian. Postage: $4.00 U.S./$5.00 Can.

[First full-length biography of this Anabaptist leader and martyr]

Pandora Press
51 Pandora Avenue N.
Kitchener, Ontario
Canada N2H 3C1
Tel./Fax: (519) 578-2381
E-mail: panpress@golden.net
Web site: www.pandorapress.com

Herald Press
616 Walnut Avenue
Scottdale, PA
U.S.A. 15683
Orders: (800) 245-7894
E-mail: hp%mph@mcimail.com
Web site: www.mph.lm.com